First publis

ISBN 1 872

CW00419986

© Chris Bar

Blorenge Cottage, Church Lane, Llanfoist, Abergavenny, Gwent NP7 9NG
Tel: 01873 856114

Printed by MWL Print Group Ltd,
Units 10/13, Pontyfelin Industrial Estate, New Inn,
Pontypool, Torfaen NP4 ODQ
Tel: 01495 750033

Photography by Chris Barber

Front Cover: Rhyd-y-meirch (Llanover Village)

Back Cover: Goose and Cuckoo Inn

"Lady Llanover left an unexpected legacy to posterity. It was her advocacy that firmly fixed the female Welsh costume into tall black steeple hats, flannel shawls and skirts - the tourist symbol of Wales!"

Wynford Vaughan-Thomas 1985

CONTENTS

"Lady Llanover might have been English by birth, and a hybrid Monmouthshire woman by adoption, but her sympathies were Welsh to the extreme, which is more than can be said of most Monmouthshire folk today, who like myself have divided loyalties between England and Wales."

Olive Phillips 1951

Launch of the Lady Llanover Society, October 2003

FOREWORD

In *Llanover Country* Chris Barber uses his extensive knowledge of the area to introduce some of the historical personalities and events, associated with the countryside surrounding Llanover.

The seven walks which are described, take one through a diverse range of landscapes and habitats, from the 'Goose & Cuckoo' up on the hill to St Bartholomews Church in Wales, through the community of Llanover and across the River Usk to Llanarth. Inbetween the walker will view traditional Beech and Larch woodland, originally grown to provide pit props for the coal mining industry, the Monmouthshire & Brecon Canal constructed to take minerals to Newport & the River Usk which flows from high in the Brecon Beacons to its confluence with the Severn Estuary. The landscape has not only been shaped by industry but also by the traditional Hill Farmers in what is now the Brecon Beacons National Park, by the Forestry Commission and by the Llanover Estate.

Chris Barber has linked the landscape with my Great-Great-Great Grandparents, Lord and Lady Llanover, who were passionate in their support for Welsh traditions, culture and language in the nineteenth century, and whose stewardship of Llanover Estate has influenced the beautiful and varied landscape which we can all enjoy today.

Elizabeth Murray

The Rhy-y-meirch flows through Llanover
to join the River Usk to the east of Llanover Park

INTRODUCTION

A few miles south of Abergavenny, in the Usk Valley is the small village of Llanover which most people only glimpse as they drive along the A4042 on their way to or from other places of greater importance. The whitewashed stone cottages give an impression of a picturesque settlement while the substantial wall surrounding Llanover Park suggests that behind it is the home of someone of note.

There is in fact a fascinating story to be told of the family who have owned and lived at Llanover since 1792. I have set out to provide the background to the story of Lord and Lady Llanover and also to describe a series of walks which people can undertake to gain an appreciation of the history and landscape of this very special locality.

In 1985 I wrote a book which paid tribute to the well known author Alexander Cordell and identified the area surrounding Blaenavon as 'Cordell Country'. In 2003 I published the first guidebook to 'Kilvert Country' which is centred on the village of Clyro in Old Radnorshire, so I have now turned my attention to creating 'Llanover Country'. There are other parts of Britain which bear such labels as 'Thomas Hardy Country', 'Wordsworth Country' or 'Catherine Cookson Country and it is an appropriate way of honouring local celebrities who have left their mark and deserve to be remembered in this way.

It is just over 200 years ago that Augusta Waddington, the future Lady Llanover was born at Llanover, where she lived all her life. She married Benjamin Hall (the third), son of a wealthy industrialist and they are both remembered for their stalwart support for preserving the Welsh language, music, culture and traditions.

Augusta participated in local eisteddfodau under her adopted bardic name of Gwenynen Gwent ('the Bee of Gwent') and from 1834 played an important part in establishing an annual eisteddfod at Abergavenny. Benjamin supported her in all her aims and he himself had a very successful career as a politician whose name was given to the famous bell known as 'Big Ben' in the clock tower of the Houses of Parliament.

My first introduction to Llanover, many years ago, was through the articles and books of Fred Hando, and as the copyright holder of his work I am pleased to include some of his relevant drawings in this publication.

Fred tells how he visited a cottage near the river to obtain the church key: "Here, huddled near a bright fire, was a sweet lady aged 91, who was introduced as Mrs Richards, and who, to our delight, proved to be none other than the once celebrated 'Pencerddes y De' - the Chief Musician of the south - a Bard in her own right.

Her father, Thomas Griffiths, although blind, from infancy, was (in1843) named Chief Harpist to King Edward VII. We listened enthralled while she told in a low musical voice of the great days when Llanover, like a magnet, drew to its great Hall and Gallery the gifted musicians of Wales."

The family harpist before Thomas Griffiths was John Jones who originated from Dolgellau. He won the silver harp, the highest award offered at the Brecon Eisteddfod and some years later became 'domestic harper' to Augusta and Benjamin Hall, remaining in their service until his early death in 1844. He is buried in Llanover Churchyard and when I sought his grave I was delighted to see that it bears the carving of a harp with 'music' symbolically emanating from it.

Llanover House, the grand home of Augusta and Benjamin was unfortunately demolished about seventy years ago and today we can only try to picture the scenes of hospitality that took place there in the 19th century.

Numerous important and influential people of the day were frequent visitors to Llanover House, such as the Rev Thomas Price ('Carnhuanawc'). Lady Charlotte Guest of Dowlais and Maria Jane Williams of Aberpergwm.

Lady Llanover outlived her husband by over twenty eight years and the heir to the estate was their only surviving child, Augusta Charlotte, who married the Llanarth Squire, John Arthur Jones; two years later the name being changed to Herbert.

Today, Elizabeth Murray, the great, great, great granddaughter of Lady Llanover is President of the 'Lady Llanover Society' which was formed in 2003 to mark the life and achievements of Augusta, first Baroness Llanover, and I am most grateful to her for writing the foreword to this book.

Chris Barber
Llanfoist
2004

1
The Waddington Family

Benjamin Waddington, son of the Rev Joshua Waddington and Ann Ferrand was born in Walkeringham, Nottinghamshire in 1749. He was brought up by his mother's great aunt, Mrs Delany, a prominent figure at the courts of George II and George III. In 1789 he married her great niece, Georgina Mary Ann Port, the daughter of John Port and Mary Dewes of Ilam in Derbyshire.

For the first two years of their married life, Benjamin and Mary Waddington lived at Dunston in Berkshire. Then in 1792 Benjamin bought the Llanover Estate in Monmouthshire. It was later commented by his daughter Frances (who later became Baroness Bunsen) that: "My father purchased, more from weariness of the long search after a dwelling, than from any temptation offered by Llanover, where an ill-built, incomplete and inelegant house needed large additions to be built in order to become a possible place of abode."

Known as Ty Uchaf (the Upper House) this property was held in the fifteenth century by Ievan ap Trahiarn ap Meurig ap Gwilym Sais ap Madog , descended from Gwaethfoed, Prince of Cardigan in the eleventh century. Jane, daughter and heir of this Ievan, married Howel, second son of Ievan ap Meurig of Penrhos and their descendants became Prichard. Barbara, only child and heir of Matthew Prichard, in about 1620, married Walter Rumsey of Usk, a Welsh judge, and took the estate to her husband.

Walter and Barbara Rumsey resided at Llanover and being an astute lawyer, Walter was known as 'the Picklock of the Law'. He succeeded Andrew Powell in 1631 as Second Justice on the Brecon Circuit of the Great Sessions of Wales (commonly known as a Welsh Judge) and held that office until 1645, when as a strong Royalist he was removed by Parliament. He was taken prisoner by the Roundheads when Hereford was captured on the 18th December 1645. At the Restoration he was named one of the knights of the intended order of the Royal Oak and died in that year, being buried in the family vault at Llanover Church, where an inscription on a pew commemorates him (see page 65). The estates of Walter Rumsey passed to the Cecil family.

When William Coxe was touring Monmouthshire in 1799, to collect material for his book entitled *A Historical Tour through Monmouthshire*. The hospitable Mr Waddington cordially invited him to stay at Llanover whilst he was exploring the surrounding area. Sir Richard Colt Hoare who illustrated the book (published in 1801) also stayed with the Waddingtons and drew a view from the Park. William Coxe described Llanover as follows:

Llanover Court Farm is a 16th century farmhouse with big chimneys and long low roofs. In the time of Elizabeth I the property belonged to the family of Ab Resort, in later years commonly called 'Richard,' of whom Matthew and William are buried at Llanover Church. The old Welsh name of this house is Cwrt y Porth-hir which refers to a one-time gateway and covered passage leading from one entrance to another but this no longer exists.

Ty Uchaf (Upper House) was once known as Dower House and also The White House. This tall, brick, Georgian building annexed to a lower and older stone house was formerly the residence of Walter Cecil, descendant of the Cecils of Allt-yr-ynys near Pandy, ancestors of the great Lord Burleigh. Walter was the last male member of the family who resided in Gwent. His coat-of-arms, elaborately carved, can be seen in Llanover Church. Augusta Waddington was born in this house in 1802. The old part of the building bears a plaque recording its 'repair' in 1742.

12

"Llanover House, the seat of Benjamin Waddington Esq., is situated to the right of the high road, nearly midway between Pont y Pool and Abergavenny. In this delightful spot I constantly experienced a kind hospitable reception, and passed much of my time during my continuance in Monmouthshire; the commodious distance from Abergavenny, Llansantfraed, Clytha, Usk, and Pont y Pool park, enabled me to enjoy the society of my friends, while I was exploring the beauties of the adjacent countryside.

The parish of Llanover, comprehending an extensive district stretches beyond Blaenavon and Pont y Pool, and is the mother church of the chapels of Trevethin, Mamhilad, and Capel Newydd.

The house stands on a gentle rise near the torrent Rhyd y Meirch, which falls from the neighbouring hills, and rippling through the grounds, hastens towards the Usk. In the front the rich meadows sink into an oval vale, intersected by the meandering Usk, and skirted by a range of gentle elevations, dotted with numerous seats, churches and hamlets; beyond these rise in a grand succession, hills and mountains which combine the varieties of light and shade, and vie in the contrast and singularity of their forms. The extremity of the vale is closed by the Clytha hills, mantled with wood; the elegant and wooded swell of the Little Skyrrid is backed by the majestic top of St Michael's Mount; the gloomy and irregular mass of the Black Mountains bound the distant horizon; to these succeed the russet summits of the Gaer and Brynaro, the four Pen y Vale Hills, which form beautiful undulations above the town of Abergavenny, and are crowned by the Sugar Loaf. Beyond the Sugar Loaf, the perspective of the Vale of Usk terminates in the rugged crags in the vicinity of Crickhowell; opposite towers the magnificent Blorenge, and joins the chain of hills which stretch to Pont y Pool."

Benjamin Waddington soon added an elegant three-storeyed red brick extension to the house and laid out the extensive gardens. In 1799 he had 120,000 larch trees brought from Glasgow and planted them at Llanover. The brook running through the grounds at that time turned a mill (long dismantled) and the new owner of Ty Uchaf formed cascades and ponds along its route. In 1800 Benjamin became High Sheriff of Monmouthshire and also spent a great deal of time transacting the business of a magistrate.

Among the close friends of the Waddington family were the Joneses, who owned the adjoining estate of Llanarth, and a branch of the same family who resided at the nearby estate of Clytha. In 1812 the Waddingtons of Llanover also became acquainted with the Halls of Abercarn.

Benjamin and Georgina Waddington had six daughters in total, but sadly only three survived. These were Frances, Emelia and Augusta and it is the latter, born at Ty Uchaf on 21 March 1802, who was in later years to become the famous Lady Llanover.

Their mother was a great believer in fresh-air and exercise, alternating with a great deal of rest. Accordingly the girls had no regular hours for lessons and no governess, being taught entirely by Mrs Waddington herself. She gave them a very sound education, out of her own extensive knowledge. The three girls studied Greek, Latin, Spanish and Italian, Euclid, economics, music, drawing, history, literature and geography, as well as the more feminine employments of embroidery and household management.

They were encouraged to draw from nature, to look at an object and plan how to draw it and to notice how the light and shade should fall. They even had to give reasons for every line that they drew. In addition they were taught the then popular art of cutting silhouettes in black paper and encouraged to read aloud and recite poetry. Later on they had lessons in music and were taught dancing by a teacher who came from Brecon.

The Six Daughters

Harriet - born and died 1790
Frances - 1791 - 1876
Mary Ann - born 1793 - died in infancy
Emilia - 1794 - 1819
Matilda - born and died 1797
Augusta - born 1802 - died 1896

Augusta (self portrait)

2
Augusta and Benjamin Hall

Augusta was only fifteen when her elder sister Frances was married in Rome to Baron Bunsen, then Prussian envoy at the papal court. Six years later in 1823, she herself was to be married to young Benjamin Hall the eldest son of Benjamin and Charlotte Hall, of Abercarn, Monmouthshire, and of Hensol Castle, Glamorgan. The Halls were gentlemen farmers who worked Daisyback Farm, Gumfreston, as had generations of Halls before them, before becoming pioneering industrialists. Charlotte was a member of the Crawshay family of Cyfartha, Merthyr Tydfil.

Benjamin was born at Hensol Castle in the Vale of Glamorgan in 1802. He was educated at Westminster School and matriculated at Christ Church Oxford. On reaching the age of twenty-one, he married Augusta Waddington. The Halls and the Waddingtons had been acquainted for many years and the fortunes of the Halls were inextricably mixed up with those of the Crawshay family, into which Benjamin Hall senior had married. He became a partner of Richard Crawshay of Cyfartha, Merthyr Tydfil in many enterprises and this is where their money came from. He was MP for Glamorganshire and his grandfather was Rev Benjamin Hall, who was Chancellor of Llandaff Cathedral.

The wedding took place in Llanover Church and the guests included Alexander Waddington, Mr and Mrs Joseph Bailey of Nantyglo, Mr Ferdinand Hanbury Williams, Mr Philip Jones of Llanarth and Mr Evans, the curate of Llanover and his wife. After the reception at about two o'clock the bride and groom set off for Trecastle in Benjamin's new carriage, drawn by four horses.

Benjamin and Augusta spent the first three years of their married life living in Newport House, Almeley, which they rented in north-west Herefordshire. They were popular with their neighbours and received invitations to dine and stay at such grand places as Kinnersley Castle and Titley Court.

Their eldest child, Augusta Charlotte Elizabeth was born on 12th September, 1824 and the second child, Benjamin Hanbury Stuart was born on 19th January 1826. There were also other children who died very young.

Four months later, the Halls left Newport House and returned to Monmouthshire, where Benjamin had by now been appointed High Sheriff. They took up residence at Abercarn House, Benjamin's mother having moved to Hampshire, and later Brighton for the sake of her health.

Settling down in the beautiful valley of the Ebbw, Benjamin devoted himself to the development of the rich mineral resources on his land.

Benjamin Hall as a young man in 1841

Opinions vary as to the height of Benjamin Hall Jnr., who was a fine figure of a man standing between 6ft 4 ins and 6ft 7 ins tall, with a well proportioned figure. Augusta on the other hand was small and dainty.

Augusta Hall (Lady Llanover) dressed in Welsh national costume

Abercarn Church was built by Sir Benjamin Hall on his estate for the sole use of Welsh speakers. It stands high above the village of Abergwyddon and was opened on 16th November 1854. Present at the opening ceremony were Sir Benjamin and Lady Hall of Llanover and some of their Welsh servants, the Rev Hugh Williams (the Welsh Chancellor of the diocese) and twenty native clergymen, the Bishop of Llandaff and the Rural Dean.

> *"Over the porch I read the stone inscription ABH 1853, indicating that the church was the joint gift of husband and wife. Inside, the impressive three decker pulpit was surmounted by a brass commemorating Lord Llanover and this like all the other inscriptions was in Welsh."*

Fred Hando 1968

18

Benjamin no doubt realised that one day he and his wife would reside at Llanover and in 1826 he bought the manor of Court Lettice, which had formerly been a part of the original manor of Llanover. Mr Waddington, when he first settled at Llanover, had tried to buy this property but without success. Two years later Benjamin bought The Mardy in part exchange for The Tandy in Goetre and, throughout his life, and that of Augusta after his death, they bought any adjoining piece of land which came on sale.

In September 1826 Benjamin, Augusta and two of her Waddington cousins, went to Brecon for the Eisteddfod. It was the first one that Augusta had ever attended and it was during this Eisteddfod that Benjamin and Augusta first heard the great harpist John Jones of Dolgellau. He won the silver harp, the highest award offered at the Brecon Eisteddfod, and some years later the Halls appointed him as their domestic harper. John Jones remained in their service until his early death in 1844.

It was also at this Eisteddfod that the Halls made the acquaintance of the Rev Thomas Price (Carnhuanawc) who had become Vicar of Llanfihangel Cwmdu in 1825. It was recorded by Carnhuanawc that this meeting was most memorable to him "as an era alike auspicious to Cambria's well-fare, and gratifying to his personal feelings... as a means of stimulating the inherent patriotism of Gwenynen Gwent (which afterwards became Augusta Hall's bardic name), and gaining for him the life-long friendship of the Llanover families."

Augusta's interest in the Welsh language received fresh inspiration from her meeting with Carnhuanawc and backed by the wealth of Benjamin Hall these three people were to do a great deal to promote a revival of Welsh language and culture.

In 1828 following the death of Benjamin Waddington the Halls moved from Abercarn to Llanover, so that Augusta could be near her mother and comfort her in her grief. It was also in this year that Benjamin Hall began building Llanover House, in the grounds of the old court, close to the boundary of Mr Waddington's estate and on the edge of a wood. He and Augusta had long planned to build a large house which would be a centre of Welsh culture. They would maintain a household harpist and endeavour to revive the old Welsh songs and dances which had been largely forgotten.

Llanover House was designed by Thomas Hopper, a successful architect who also built Penrhyn Castle in North Wales for G.H. Dawkins-Pennant a year earlier. He had also reconstructed Margam Abbey in Glamorganshire for the Talbots. Work started on Llanover House in February 1828 and it took nine years to complete the building. While one writer considered the building to be a model for beauty of design and proportion, another described it as a 'vast Gothic monstrosity'. Yet this was

Born in 1788, the son of the Vicar of Pencaerebin in Llanfihangel Bryn Pabau, near Builth Wells, Thomas Price was ordained in 1811 and two years later he moved to Crickhowell to take charge of the parishes of Llangenny, Llanbedr Ystradyw and Partrishow. To these in 1816 were added the neighbouring parishes of Llangattock and Llanelly. Early in 1825 he received the vicarage of Llanfihangel Cwmdu, augmented in 1839 by the curacy of Tretower.

The Rev Thomas Price was also known by his bardic name of Carnhuanawc and he did much for the development of Welsh art and literature. He was a prose writer, bard, harpist, orator and a pioneer of Welsh renaissance. He was the principal supporter of Lady Llanover in founding The Literary Society of the Cymreigyddion at Abergavenny in 1833 and also in founding the Welsh Manuscripts Society.

His eloquent speeches were a prominent feature at the various eisteddfodau and he won prizes for his essays on Celtic history. (Undoubtedly) 'Carnhuanawc was recognised as one of the most foremost scholars of his day.

hardly fair for he had not actually seen it! Photographs taken from various angles during its great days show that it was in fact a plain dignified Jacobean style building.

The mansion was built of sandstone extracted from the local hills and it contained a music gallery, elaborately carved in chestnut wood and decorated with gilding. The mantelpieces of the main apartments were all specimens of the marbles of South Wales. All the rooms were expensively furnished for Benjamin Hall was indeed a very wealthy man. An inlaid table standing in the centre of the hall was made from part of the famous Golynos oak which stood just outside Newport. Rated as the largest oak tree in Britain it was felled in 1810. Throughout the mansion there was a great deal of oak panelling and some 6,000 feet square of polished oak flooring

It was the Halls' desire that their grand mansion should be a centre of Welsh culture and on its completion in 1837 a house warming party, culminating in a large fancy-dress ball was held there to mark the end of the Abergavenny Eisteddfod of that year. This was the first of many successive glittering house parties which were held for that purpose until the society of Cymreigyddion y Fenni was dissolved in January 1854.

Llanover House was built within 400 yards of Ty Uchaf
on the Llanover boundary of the Park Lettice property
purchased by Benjamin Hall in 1826

Porthmawr was built by Benjamin Hall to form a ceremonial entrance to the drive leading to the new Llanover House

Benjamin Hall modelled his main gateway entrance to the drive leading to Llanover House on Porthmawr at Crickhowell which had been constructed by the Herberts during the time of the Tudors.

Above the archway on each side of the Llanover Porth Mawr, Benjamin Hall had inscriptions carved on slabs of stone which addressed the guests who were arriving and also departing. The inscriptions in Welsh have now unfortunately weathered away, but once read:

> 'Pwy wyt Ddyfodwr?
> Os cyfaill, croeso cabu iti:
> Os diethr, Lletty garwch a'therys:
> Os gelyn, Addfwynder a´´garchara
>
> Ymadawydd hynaws, gad fendith
> Ar dy ol; a bendithier dithau;
> Iechyd a hoen it' ar y daith,
> A dedwydd ddychweliad. '

Translated they once read:

Entrance side

> 'Who art thou comer?
> If a friend, the welcome of the heart to thee:
> If a stranger hospitality shall meet thee:
> If an enemy, courtesy shall imprison thee.'

Exit side

> 'Departing guest, leave a blessing
> On thy footsteps , and May'st thou be blessed:
> Health and prosperity be with thee on thy journey
> And happiness on thy return.'

These verses were the winning entry for an Eisteddfod competition set by Lady Llanover.

"When we entered the Park through Porth Mawr, the name of one of the Lodges, I was very amused to see the women who were brushing the walks dressed in hats and bob tails and stuff aprons etc."

Margaret Davies 1861

Porth y Gwenynen is the entrance on the road from Llanover to Llanvair and it was built and named in honour of Lady Llanover, whose bardic name was Gwenynen Gwent ('The Bee of Gwent')

Llanover House had a life of 107 years and it was demolished in 1935, having become unstable due to the soft, porous sandstone used in its construction, and many years of neglect. It was last inhabited in 1911 by Augusta Herbert. The late Lord Treowen had rarely used it, preferring to reside at Llanarth Court.

3
Life at Llanover House

Augusta's cousin Horace Waddington spent the New Year at Llanover in 1859 and described his visit in his diary as follows:

"In the magnificent house built in the park some little way from the old 'White House' - the arrangement of the household was quaint, maids in old-fashioned style with white crossovers, early dinner at two (announced by the butler in Welsh) high tea in the dining-room at eight. Lady Hall took me all round the grounds, shrubberies, the seven springs of St Gofer, the Cromlech, and then the walled gardens, hot-houses, etc., and I saw the famous old giant rhododendron about 85 paces round. On Sunday morning Sir Benjamin and I went to the English services in the little church, in the afternoon Lady Hall to the Welsh service, she in strict Welsh dress - pointed tall hat with feather and close frilled cap under it, scarlet mantle fur-bordered and a shortish skirt. She always spoke Welsh with her servants - she had her family harpist, old Griffith, who was a celebrated player of the old triple-stringed Welsh harp - a most difficult art as instead of putting the single row of strings into different keys by the pedals, each tone and half tone had its own string; he used to come in of an evening, in the gallery of the great hall, to play to us delightfully, old Welsh airs... Lady Hall was so active that her bardic name of Gwenynen Gwent - the bee of Gwent - was singularly apposite. I was driven out to see the great places round about - Llanarth, Clytha, the Hendre, Raglan etc., and was sent shooting on my own in the coverts with keepers and dogs - including old Lewis aged 80, head-keeper, who remembered my father there as a youngster before he went to India in 1813. Lewis had been fifty years in the family, originally as butler to old Mr Benjamin Waddington (Horace's great-uncle). Later in the year and in 1860 I used to visit the Llanovers at their fine London house - 9 Great Stanhope Street."

Christmas at Llanover House was a very special occasion. The great hall was beautifully decorated with holly, mistletoe and other evergreens. A huge bell was rung to summon the tenants to dinner with the long tables laden with shoulders of mutton, baked, boiled or roasted rounds of beef weighing between 24 and 38 lbs each, 7 geese, giblet pies, 240 mince pies from a special Llanover recipe, rice puddings, apple pies etc., oranges, ginger-breads, apples and nuts. Lavish helpings were also sent to those who were too old or ill to come to the house.

While the meal was being digested, the household harpist played and the more gifted servants and tenants sang to his accompaniment, after which prizes were presented for a wide range of competitions.

These included awards for the best flocks of Welsh sheep (black or white); best turnips and other vegetables; the best whitewashed cottage and the best gardens of flowers or vegetables.

A tea party was then held for the children with plenty of cakes and jellies. Dancing began at 6 pm and the Welsh jigs, reels and folk-dances with intervals for singing, went on until midnight.

St David's Day was another special occasion, with Leek Broth, Leeks on Toast and Toasted Cheese as the traditional dishes. There was harp-playing and singing, a St David's Day dinner and everyone wore leeks or daffodils. The guests were bidden to dinner with a call from the butler: "Mae'r ciniaw yn barod!" (Dinner's ready!).

In June, when the Llanover rhododendrons were in bloom, there was a garden party for the tenants to which the tradesmen of Abergavenny and their families were also invited. Tents were set up in the grounds and there was lavish provision of refreshments followed by sports, music and dancing.

Lord and Lady Llanover were friends of Queen Sophie of Holland, the first wife of King Wilhelm III and they entertained her at their London house, when she was in England. Her eldest son, the Prince of Orange, stayed with them at Llanover in 1860.

On his arrival in London, the young Prince was escorted by Lord Llanover to the Houses of Parliament and other places of interest in the city. He then travelled to Wales and first went to Troy House, near Monmouth, where he was received by the Duke of Beaufort, who escorted him to Raglan Castle. Here they were joined by Lord Llanover and Mr Herbert of Llanarth. After inspecting the ruins, they drove to Llanarth for luncheon and then went on to Llanover. The next day the Prince was taken to see Crumlin Viaduct, the Cyfartha Works and Cyfartha Castle at Merthyr Tydfil and then back to Llanover.

In the evening a banquet was held in his honour and this was followed by a variety of entertainment. The Llanover Cantorion sang Welsh songs, Gruffydd played on his triple harp and the servants danced Welsh reels and jigs. On Sunday the Prince attended a Welsh service at Llanover church and left the next day to visit Hereford Cathedral, Chester and Bangor.

The old stable block, just north of the mansion site, is in a derelict condition. The entrance is through a Tudor style gateway with side turrets topped with stone caps and large metal weathervanes. This building was certainly an impressive sight for visitors arriving in their carriages down the driveway leading through the park from Porth Mawr.

In a grove of hollies are nine wells in a circle - the united waters of which fall over two basins into a bath. The largest well is known as Ffynnon Gover 'the well of Gover' after whom Llanover is named. The wells are supposed to have healing virtues. It has eight surrounding wells, all flowing in different ways, but uniting in a bath. The drawing is by Lady Llanover.

The Dovecote

The Rhyd-y-meirch flows through the grounds of Llanover Park

The entrance to the Park in Llanover village is called Porth y Pentre - the 'Village Gateway' and it leads to Ty Uchaf which was formerly the residence of Walter Cecil, the descendant of the Sysyllts.

The flock of Black Welsh Mountain sheep which can be seen in Llanover Park are directly descended from those brought here by Lady Llanover from West Wales in 1840. Determined to preserve all things Welsh, she believed that sheep should be black like the Welsh cattle. In her cookery book, Lady Llanover mentions that the wool from these sheep is of 'very fine quality' and stockings knitted of the wool were 'very superior and did not need any dye'. This is one of the oldest pedigree flocks of Black Welsh Mountain sheep in existence.

4
Llanover Village

"Every house, every cottage, is in the best style of the age which produced it. The buildings are of whitewashed stone hewn from the neighbouring mountains, with woodwork of local larch and oak, and roofs of slate or stone."

Arthur Mee 1951

Llanover is a much dispersed settlement with the old village and the parish church stretching along the banks of the River Usk. Llanover Fawr comprises the old parishes of Llanover, Llandewi Rhydderch, Llangattock-nigh-Usk, Llanvihangel-nigh-Usk, Llansantffraed and Llanvair Kilgeddin. The parish is divided into upper and lower divisions, the former being mainly mountain land. The lower part of the parish at one time was known as Llanover Dyfnwal after Dyfnwal ap Caradwg, the lord of the district in the twelfth century.

The main part of the village is called Rhyd-y-meirch and this is what most people know today as Llanover. It lies on the west side of the A4042, with Llanover Park enclosed by walls on the opposite side of the road.

There was a time when the main road did not exist and in front of the Gwesty was a ford called Rhyd-y-meirch ('Ford of the Stallions'). This stream passes under the road and re-emerges in the park.

Seven pubs were once in business on the Llanover Estate. They were called Pen Ceffyl (the former post office in Llanover), Pen Gofrlwyd, Gwesty, Ty'r Eos, Seren Gobaith, Pen Groes Oped and The Lion. Determined to keep her tenants sober,Lady Llanover, who was a fervent teetotaller, purchased all these pubs and either turned them into coffee taverns or private houses. The only pub that escaped is the one situated on the hillside above the village which rejoices in the splendid name 'The Goose and Cuckoo'. The teetotal views of Lord and Lady Llanover led to a local rhyme:

> *Grand House but small cheer*
> *Large cellar but no beer*
> *Lord Llanover lives here.*

Lady Llanover expected her tenants and workers to abstain from drink at all times and when she saw the bicycle of one of her gardeners leaning against the wall of the Waun y Clare Inn near Mamhilad, she made a point of rebuking him the following day. His cheeky response was to leave his bicycle one night beneath her bedroom window!

A Calvinistic Methodist cause was supported for many years by Lady Llanover with services held in Ty Uchaf and in a large room at the Gwesty Dirwestl. But when the congregation became too large for these places Lady Llanover erected a chapel of galvanized iron, which after her death, was replaced by a stone building endowed by her will.

The first minister to be appointed was the Rev George Erskine Watson, the son of Rev William Watson who died at Kenfig Hill, Glamorganshire in 1872. The Rev George Watson came to Llanover in 1878 but soon afterwards went to Lady Llanover's chapel at Abercarn where he died in 1884. The next minister was the Rev. Thomas Miles, a native of Dinas Powis in Glamorganshire, who went to America in 1884 and was succeeded by the Rev. John Prys, a native of Llanwrtyd in Breconshire.

Lady Llanover endowed the Rhydermeirch Calvinistic Methodist Chapel, stipulating that the pastor had to be bearded! Services were conducted in Welsh but with a liturgy based on the Book of Common Prayer.

Hanover Chapel

At a corner of the village can be found Hanover Chapel which was built in 1839. The nearby minister's cottage was the original chapel, and under the scullery floor lies Rees Davies who died in 1767 after being minister here for 43 years. In the graveyard rests Emmanuel Davies who died in 1838 after serving as minister for 48 years.

The Congregational cause at Hanover is one of the oldest in Monmouthshire, being the third in direct lineal descent from Llanvaches, the mother-church of Nonconformity in Wales. As far back as 1662 it is mentioned, in conjunction with other churches at Usk, Llangwm, Llantrisant and Llangibby, as forming an off-shoot of Llanvaches. It was located then in the parish of Goytre, at a farmhouse called Abergwenllan. Here preaching services were held for many years until the first chapel was built in 1744. It was built in the parish of Llanover and called Hanover, probably in honour of the reigning sovereign. In 1839 the old meeting-house, having become too small for the congregation, was incorporated with the manse and the present chapel was erected close by at a cost of £500. On April 16 and 17 1840 the opening services took place with no less than ten preachers participating.

Fifty years later the brotherhood at Hanover were of the opinion that the chapel required a complete renovation to bring its internal structure into harmony with the architectural taste of the age. Plans were submitted and the contract was entrusted to Mr Roberts a builder at Llanelen. The work was completed by March 29th 1893 at a cost of £300 and the opening services were held.

The second Hanover Chapel opened in 1840

A memorial inside the chapel commemorates Robert Jermain Thomas, the son of a minister here. He sailed for Shanghai as a missionary in 1863, but soon afterwards his wife died. He then went to Korea, making many friends there before going on to Peking to take charge of the London Missionary Society's school.

In 1866 there was a rising against the Christians in Korea and some French missionaries were murdered. Robert decided to try to help the situation in this country that he had come to love and he sailed there in the American schooner named the *General Sherman*. On the way up the Tai Tong River, whenever the ship went near enough to the bank, he threw copies of the Bible in Korean to the people watching.

Unfortunately, when the ship anchored, fighting began and all the sailors were massacred. Robert Thomas, throwing his remaining Bibles ashore, waded to the beach with one in his hands and offered it to a Korean soldier. The man refused it, and the young missionary knelt down to pray. Then, smiling, he again offered the book but the soldier dealt him a death blow.

But Robert Thomas did not die in vain, for the Bibles that he had thrown ashore were used to paper the walls of Korean houses. In due course the strange writings were read and studied and the Koreans became interested in Christianity. There is even a chapel in the city of Pyeng Yang built in the memory of Robert Jermain Thomas of Llanover.

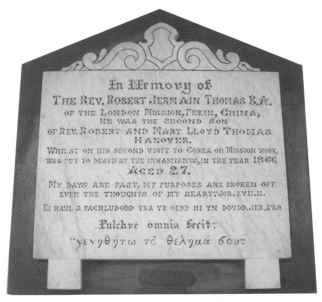

Memorial to Robert Jermain Thomas

The Gwesty Dirwestol (Temperance Hotel) was previously an inn named 'The Old Duke'. After its conversion the room on the first floor, running the whole length of the house, was used by Lady Llanover for her May Fair - 'Ffair Facy y Gwesty' - held each year on May 14th.

Rhyd-y-meirch Mill, Llanover is now a private house

This rare survival of a circular pig-sty in the garden of 'Well Cottage' was built in the 19th century.

Beside the A4042 is this drinking trough for horses, providing a reminder of the days when the horse played a vital role in everyday life

The Rhyd-y-meirch flows through the village

Powered by the waters of the Rhyd-y-meirch, the Gwenffrwd woollen mill was set up by Lady Llanover for the purpose of weaving traditional Welsh flannel. The Welsh woolen industry is based on a very ancient craft going back several centuries. Many of the first factories were run by water power and some of the woollen mills still surviving are situated next to fast flowing streams.

The Mari Lwyd

Every year on New Year's Eve, the young men of the village would obtain the skull of a horse, or perhaps make one out of wood. It was mounted on a pole about five feet tall and enveloped in a white sheet. Pieces of black cloth were sewn onto the sheet to represent ears and two black bottles were inserted into the sockets of the skeleton's head to serve as eyes. The sheet was also decorated with pink, blue and yellow ribbons. A man stood under the sheet, and held the pole supporting the head. He caused the grotesque horse to make terrifying snapping sounds, either by means of a wooden clapper or by clicking the lower jaw into which a spring had been inserted.

A merry crowd of villagers would carry this magical creation around the houses. The man who guided the horse with a pair of reins acted as the leader and when they reached a dwelling which they intended to enter, he banged on the door with a stick.

The Mari Lwyd party then sang verses which those inside had to answer. When at last the door was opened, everyone would dance inside accompanied by the Mari Lwyd. The horse would then chase young girls around the room with loud neighing noises causing much screaming and hearty laughter. After a dance and the enjoyment of food and drink, the merry gang would depart, singing a song of thanks and shouting good wishes to their hosts.

It would seem that the origins of the Mari Lwyd go back to very early times and it may well have begun as a pre-Christian ceremony, which was later taken over by the Church and turned into a cult connected with the Virgin Mary. It is probable that after the Reformation, all references to the Virgin were excluded.

There is a legend that the Mari Lwyd represents the horse that was turned out of its stable so that Christ could be laid in the manger at Bethlehem, and ever since, the horse has been looking for shelter.

Traditional Verses

"Well here we are coming
Good friends on a mission
We ask for permission to sing
If we don't get permission
O tell us by singing
Where we should be winging tonight

We've broken our shins
By climbing o'er stiles
And we have walked miles this night."

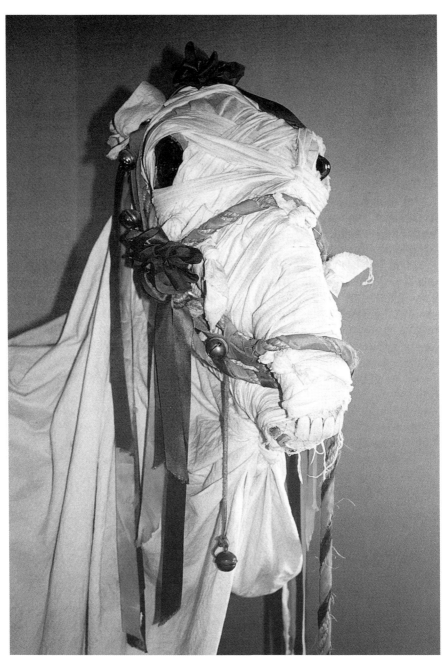

This example of a Mari Lwyd was photographed
at Rhosilli Visitor Centre, Gower, West Wales

This painting of the Mari Lwyd which can be seen above the entrance to the former Llanover Post Office was painted at the request of Lady Llanover in about 1860, to illustrate an old Welsh custom which once prevailed in many parts of Wales. The painting shows the front of Llanover House in the light of a crescent moon. A man stands by the side of the figure who wears the 'horse's head' and he is the leader of the party. When Llanover House was sold in 1834, Lot 52 in the catalogue was 'two carved wood horses heads.'

The Mari Lwyd at Llanover Post Office
Sketched by Fred Hando in 1950

41

Llanover School

The first reference to a school in Llanover is found in the parish register of 1776. Lessons were held in the tower of the parish church. It was Benjamin Hall who in 1835 built the first regular school which was made available to children of all denominations and the teaching was of a high standard. A Mr Morris was schoolmaster in 1837, next came Mr Jones of the Vro and in 1838, the Rev John Evans, vicar of Llanover took charge. In 1842 a Welsh bard called Brychan Bach was appointed. Five years later, John Powell became schoolmaster and he was paid by Lady Llanover, a salary of £15 per annum, with a cottage rent free and what children's fees he could collect. William Hopcyn became master in 1870 on a salary of £26, to rise by £10; and his accommodation was free, and again he could collect the children's fees. When he retired he was granted a pension of £20 per annum, by Lady Llanover for life. John Davies, a certified master was then appointed. By 1897 there was a total of 97 children on the books, of whom 62 were from Llanover, 62 from Goytre and 11 from Llanelen.

Every year there was a prize for the boy who spoke the best Welsh. In addition an annual prize of Welsh costumes was given to pupils for their knowledge of Welsh customs. It must have been very exciting for the children to see Lady Llanover driving up to the school in her carriage and four with coachmen, footmen and postillion, in the Llanover livery of chocolate and brown to present the prizes.

The school was continued till 1870, wnen under the Act of that year it was taken over by the County Education Department. The building is now a private house known as Yr Hen Ysgoldy (The Old School).

Lady Llanover's grandson Major General Sir Ivor Herbert (later Lord Treowen) built the present school in 1925 and named it Ysgol Tre Elidyr in memory of his gallant son, Captain Elidyr Herbert who was killed in the First World War. As well as the name, the school motto is cut on the elegant stone front - 'Ysgol Harddwch Gwlad' (School in beautiful country).

About forty years ago the Gwent historian Fred Hando paid a visit to Llanover school to see a fascinating collection of relics gathered together from around the village and the following extracts from his subsequent article make interesting reading:

"In the big light classroom the fifty children were excited as the visitors inspected their exhibits. From cottage mantelpieces, from attics and glory holes, from stables and sheds, and sometimes from secret treasure-hides, the relics had been brought. Mr Rist and Miss Violet Bracey (his assistant) were both thrilled as the children. Listen in as they show me around:

"Do these say anything to you? 'Two Little Girls in Blue', 'Happy Dreams', 'Jubilee Waltz', 'Soldiers' Dreams' - each with its heart-throb cover. Here are a shawl and blanket woven at Gwenffrwd, and here are bobbins from the same mill. Would you like two of our girls to dress in the costumes of the 1860's?"

Within a few minutes two quietly pretty girls, Ann Saunders and Pamela Jones, came shyly into the room displaying clothes made from Lady Llanover's sheep's wool at Gwenffrwd. Let Welsh showmen take a tip from Llanover; Welsh homespun needs the unsophisticated beauty of Llanover girls to show it at its best."

"Costumes like these were worn on the great occasions at Llanover," continued Miss Bracey, *"and in costumes like these the Llanover Reel was danced in the Great Hall. How were the men dressed? Come over here."*

She passed to me a pair of men's plush 'sailor-fronted' breeches, walnut-brown in blue, an attractive red and black check waistcoat, and a grey flannel frock coat. I was forced to conclude that men's dress clothes of today lack the panache and appeal of those colourful days.

On we went: "Here is a spring-balance weighing by ounces up to 30 lb.; here worn on a chain around the neck, a lady's ornament comprising button-hook, penknife and pencil; that is a pint cider mug of 1780, this is a glazed earthenware brandy bottle and here is a medicine glass with the measures etched.

We have this set of coronation mugs from Queen Victoria to Elizabeth II, and one fine diamond jubilee mug of 1897."

"The brass alphabet includes, you will note, the ampersand and the dipthong CE. That dates from 1729. Half sovereigns and sovereigns were weighed accurately on this brass balance, and if your cork-screw drove the cork into the bottle it could be retrieved by this cork-remover.

We have many portions of harness as you see, but for us this portrait of Grufydd the Harpist, and these horse-brasses for 'Lester' and 'Capten',' the horses used by Jones the Waggoner, take pride of place. Here are his gaiters."

There was much more but there I must stop."

"SCHOOL ALPHABET.
ST. PAUL'S. 1729."

LLANOVER
COSTUMES
of 1860
(from a photograph.)

43

Ysgol Tre Elidyr was built by Sir Ifor Herbert in 1925

Two benches made by sculptor Neil Gow in 2002 to celebrate the 200th anniversary
of the birth of Lady Llanover can be seen in the garden of Llanover Primary School.
This one bears the face of Lady Llanover

On this upright seat can be seen the face of Lord Llanover. Both seats are engraved with the words 'Ysgol Tre Elidyr 2002 ' and they were officially unveiled by Elizabeth Murray of Llanover Estate, which donated the sweet chestnut wood out of which they were carved.

Tre Elidyr (Elidyr's Town)

Today, the core of the housing in Llanover is the model village of Tre Elidyr, the whole of which is a unique memorial to soldiers killed in the First World War. It was conceived by Lord Treowen, whose son and heir, Captain Elidyr Herbert, was killed on 17th November 1917, during active service in Palestine.

The designer was Alfred H. Powell (who was an associate of Ernest Gimson) and originally twenty houses were planned but only eighteen were built before Lord Treowen's own death. The last two were built at a later date. Seeking a nucleus, Alfred Powell took two large oak trees standing about the middle of the site between two fields in a hedgerow running at right angles to the main Abergavenny road, and made them the centre of the village green. This square of 185 feet each way is bisected by a footpath passing under these oaks with one end upon the road and the other entry opposite the school.

The houses surround a large village green on which stands the war memorial. This is a slim monolith 11 feet tall, surmounted by a gilded iron cross (made by a local blacksmith). Large blocks of unhewn rock were placed around the base to form steps. and behind it is a wall bearing three brass plaque which are inscribed with the names of those who died in the Great War. Around the memorial is a semi-circle of lime trees, one planted for each man who died.

5
A Hotbed of Welshness

"For passionate commitment to Wales nobody could beat Lady Llanover, neé Augusta Waddington. Though she lived in a heavily Anglicised part of Wales, near Abergavenny (Y Fenni) in Gwent, Lady Llanover turned her mansion and estate into a very hotbed of Welshness."

Jan Morris 1984

Lady Llanover had an enthusiasm for all things Welsh and made sure that all the houses of the Llanover Estate had Welsh names and that the agricultural workers and domestic servants all spoke Welsh. In addition she did her best to revive the manufacture in Gwent of Welsh flannel; invented a Welsh costume and insisted that all her house-servants wore it.

Throughout the Victorian era the people of Wales were rapidly shedding all the customs and domestic traditions of their ancestors. To stem this national *degrinolade* Lady Llanover set her example of old-time practice at Llanover. But her ideas were not always accepted with enthusiasm by the genuine Welshmen and Welshwomen they were intended to attract.

Persons more conversant with the Welsh language than Lady Llanover, who only "spoke Welsh pretty well for a foreigner," were sometimes irritated by being compelled to carry on a halting conversation in Welsh with their hostess.

The countryside around Llanover was wholly anglicised and Lady Llanover met this difficulty by importing a number of monoglot Welsh-speaking Methodists from North Cardiganshire and their pastor with them. This quite naturally did not please the local vicar, with whom her Ladyship quickly fell out.

Her circle of lady friends who regularly visited Llanover House included the poet/historian, Jane Williams of Talgarth, Maria Jane Williams of Aberpergwm, who won an eisteddfod prize for her collection of Welsh airs and Lady Charlotte Guest who is famous for her translation of the 'Mabinogion'.

Augusta was very fond of music and a harpist was always resident in the house to play the triple stringed harp and to instruct others in the art. The harp has been played in Wales since the age of the Welsh Princes when a harpist was an essential member of the household. The art of singing to the harp is known as 'Canu Pennillion'.

The harpist plays a harmonised setting of a Welsh air, and keeps on playing as if the singer were not there, repeating it several times without a break. The singer chooses the words and sings them in a descant to the air. The descant may be one he or she has learnt or one made up. The words may be traditional verses, joyful or satirical or love poems.

In July 1843, John Jones, the Llanover harpist and Thomas Gruffydd (then harpist at Tredegar) were invited to accompany the Rev Thomas Price, who was taking a triple harp to London to be presented to the Prince of Wales. All three visited Buckingham Palace where the two great harpists played on the Prince's harp and upon their own instruments, much to the delight of the Royal family.

Thomas Gruffydd lived for the greater part of his life at Llanover as the resident harpist. He came from Llangynidr originally and was blind from childhood as the result of an accident. Known as Cerddor y Dwyrain, he was a very skilled harpist and won many prizes at Eisteddfodau. In 1869 he played by command before Queen Victoria at Buckingham Palace and at Marlborough House before the Prince of Wales, by whom he was appointed 'Welsh Harper Extraordinaire to his Royal Highness'.

The triple-stringed harp is a complex instrument which was known as Delyn-Deir-Rhes. In 1913 the Rev. Ceitho Davies commented:

"It has considerable advantages from a musical point of view over the pedal instrument. Its tone, for one thing, is rich because of the open string for all notes and the beautiful effects of the unison notes of the two diatronic scales are unique. These effects cannot be produced on any other existing instrument, whilst for perfection of tone the old triple harp cannot be surpassed in the hands of a skilled performer. In addition to all this, its price is moderate, for it can be built at half the cost of the pedal harp."

Dorothy Eastwood in her book, River Diary, published in 1950, describes meeting at Pant-y-goitre, a 95 year-old woman whose father had been a Llanover harpist in the late 19th century. She herself had also played the harp for Lady Llanover and commented:

"She was one of the first people to collect and preserve the old Welsh songs, although in those days it was thought a ridiculous thing to do. But she persevered, and later other people began collecting them too, but it was late then, and many of them were lost."

Although all the best-known Welsh harpists and musicians of the eighteenth century collected and published Welsh airs, it was not until 1844 that the first official collection was made by Jane Williams of Aberpergwm. Lady Hall generously contributed towards the cost of publishing the collection under the title of *Ancient National Airs of Gwent and Morgannwg*. Jane Williams had recorded every air in the collection from folk singers in all parts of South Wales and in particular from the Vale of Neath. The collection won her a prize at the Abergavenny Eisteddfod of 1837.

It was largely through the efforts of the Llanovers that Abergavenny became an important centre in the movement to revive Welsh culture and an annual eisteddfod, followed by a dinner at the Angel Hotel was held in the town for 21 years.

On 22nd November 1833, a meeting of some twenty-five Monmouthshire gentlemen had taken place at the Sun Inn in Abergavenny, and it was decided to form a new Welsh Literary Society to be called Cymdeithas Cymreigyddion y Fenni. Mr Evans, Vicar of Llanover was appointed President and it was agreed that he should invite Mr and Mrs Hall to become members. They were delighted to be asked and joined the Society without hesitation.

It was not long before seventy-five members had been enrolled and these included such distinguished people as Sir Charles Morgan of Tredegar, Mr Williams of Llangybi and Sir John and Lady Charlotte Guest of Dowlais. The Society would aim to urge the teaching of Welsh to children, not only in Sunday Schools but also in the day schools, to encourage Welsh people to give Welsh names to their children and to hold competitions in Welsh poetry, prose, singing and harp-playing. It was largely due to the Abergavenny Society that others sprang up all over Wales and that the Welsh language survived at all.

In August 1834, Augusta competed in the Cardiff Eisteddfod under the name of 'Gwenynen Gwent' (the Busy Bee of Gwent), and won a prize for her essay *On the advantages of preserving the language and dress of Wales*. The essay was written in English, there being no requirement at that time for everything to be in Welsh. She was admitted under her bardic name in the following Autumn as an Ovate to the Gorsedd of Bards, at a meeting held near Pontypridd.

In due course her essay was published with a series of coloured illustrations of Welsh costumes, painted in watercolours by Augusta herself. In later years the illustrations were reproduced by the National Library of Wales in a series of twelve postcards.

Lady Llanover commented in her essay:

"... on the advantages resulting from the preservation of the Costumes of the Principality, which of late years have fallen greatly into dis-use through the discouragement they have met from the higher orders, who, nevertheless, at the present time are frequently known to lament this circumstance, and to regret and deprecate the introduction of foreign luxuries in articles of dress. The costumes of Wales being chiefly composed of wool, are from the nature of the material particularly well adapted to defend the wearer against the inclemencies of the weather, and the sudden transitions from heat to cold to which our climate is subject..."

"Her great idea is Wales - that is she lives in Wales, and that the people must be kept Welsh, and that she has Welsh schools, a Welsh harper, Welsh services, always talks Welsh to her servants and wears a Welsh costume at church."

Agustus Hare 1877

> *"How frequently do we now see the hale and robust mother of fifty and even grandmother of eighty, returning from church or market secure from the storm, under the protection of the warm woollen gown, and comfortable cloak or whittle of Gwent or Dyfed, with a neat and serviceable beaver hat, and black woollen stockings pursuing her homeward path and unobstructed by the influence of cold or wet, while the delicate and cotton clad daughter or grand-daughter with perhaps the symptoms of consumption on her cheek is shivering in the rain, seeking the precarious shelter of the nearest hedge or shifting her station from tree to tree, to avoid the soaking of the shower, while her flimsy straw bonnet, saturated with water, and dyed like a rainbow, by the many coloured streams, descending from its numerous and once gaudy ribbons, is presenting a deplorable example of the sad effects resulting from that absurd abandonment of wise habits."*

Augusta won a prize of a Seal Ring with a Welsh Motto engraved on a Welsh Pebble. Value £1 10s.

The Cardiff Eisteddfod turned out to be the last of the Provincial Eisteddfodau in South Wales and their place was taken by Eisteddfodau arranged by Cymreigyddion y Fenni at Abergavenny. They held their first Eisteddfod in November 1834 and it was one of a series known as Eisteddfodau y Fenni, held annually for the next five years.

Benjamin Hall presided over the Eisteddfod held in October 1837 and among those present was Ioan Tegid, who had recently transcribed the *Red Book of Hergest* for Lady Charlotte Guest and otherwise helped her with the translations of *The Mabinogion*.

Under the joint planning of the Rev. Thomas Price (Carnhuanawc) and Lady Hall (Gwenynen Gwent), the Abergavenny Eisteddfodau grew so popular that a special Cymreigyddion Hall was built in Tudor Street. It was opened with great ceremony in 1845, under the presidency of Sir Benjamin Hall. All the Eisteddfodau of the Society were brilliant events, and also drew scholars from England, Brittany and Germany. The Society continued until 1854, when on the 14th January, Cymreigyddion y Fenni was dissolved. During its twenty-one years of existence it had revived interest in the Welsh language and culture to such an extent that other societies sprang up all over the country.

The Abergavenny Eisteddfodau did much to foster the growth of national consciousness, which led in a few years to the demand for national institutions, a National Museum, a National Library and a National University. In 1858, the Eisteddfod itself became a national institution. A clergyman from North Wales, John Williams (ab Ithel), a friend of Lady Llanover, was present at the Abergavenny Eisteddfod of 1853. He was so impressed by what he saw there that he subsequently became mainly responsible for turning the Llangollen Eisteddfod of 1858 into a national gathering.

The 1845 Eisteddfod at Abergavenny took place on the 15th and 16th of October in the newly erected Cymreigyddion Hall in Tudor Street. This was the largest public building in Monmouthshire, with a platform and gallery and small adjacent rooms. It was lavishly decorated with Welsh emblems, and thronged with bards and women in Welsh costumes. The Hall was opened with great ceremony under the presidency of Sir Benjamin Hall.

In 1861 Lady Llanover edited *The Autobiography of Mrs Delany* (Mary Granville), a work in six bulky volumes, which throws light on the leading characters of the Georgian era. From Mrs Delany, Lady Llanover had inherited the ten volumes known as *Flora Delanica*. This collection was a series of paper cut-out flowers in minute detail, and carried out by Mrs Delany in what she called 'paper mosaic'. The botanical accuracy is quite amazing, and the whole collection was left by Lady Llanover to the British Museum.

Her book *The First Principles of Good Cookery and Recipes communicated by the Hermit of the Cell of St Gover* is a 480 page volume published in 1867. The text is written in a form of dialogue between 'The Hermit of St Gover' and 'The Traveller', who is a visitor to Wales. In the introduction Lady Llanover states: "My aim has been to preserve or restore all the good old habits of my country, and utterly repudiate all immoral introductions which ruin the health as well as imperil the soul.."

Welsh Toasted Cheese

Welsh toasted cheese and the melted cheese of England are as different in the mode of preparation as the cheese itself. Cut a slice of the real Welsh cheese made of sheep's and cow's milk, toast it at the fire on both sides, but not so much as to drop: toast a piece of bread, less than a quarter of an inch thick, to be quite crisp, and spread it very thinly with fresh cold butter on one side (it must not be saturated with butter) and lay the toasted cheese upon the bread and serve immediately upon a very hot plate.

Short Cakes of Gwent and Morganwg

One pound of flour, three ounces of currants well picked and washed, a little sugar (and spice if liked): mix into a thick batter with one pint of sheep's milk cream, butter the tin of a Dutch oven and drop it in and bake before the fire. Care must be taken in turning; it can be cut in any shape. Cream of cow's milk may be used but sheep's milk cream is best for these cakes.

Welsh Salt Duck

For a common sized duck, a quarter of a pound of salt to be well rubbed and re-rubbed, and turned on a dish every day for three days, then wash all the salt off clean, put it in a 'double' with half a pint of water to the pound and let it simmer steadily for two hours. hours."

Lady Llanover helped to initiate the Welsh Manuscript Society which has long been extinct, but while it existed did much good work. The most important volumes published were the *Liber Landavensis* (1840), transcribed and translated by the Rev William Jenkins Rees, rector of Cascob in Radnorshire; the Iolo MSS (1848); *The Cambro-British Saints* (1853), *The Literature of the Kymru* by Thomas Stephens and *Ancient and National Airs of Gwent* by Jane Williams

Lady Llanover's friend, Lady Charlotte Guest, wife of the Welsh industrial magnate, Sir Josiah Guest and a daughter of the ninth Earl of Lindsey was just a few years younger than Lady Llanover. She was most probably moved by the appeal and example from Gwent to study the literature of medieval Wales, with the result that a fine edition of the Mabinogion and a good English translation of these ancient Welsh tales were published.

6
Benjamin Hall, Distinguished Whig Politician

"Benjamin Hall, the grandson of the first Richard Crawshay and as a Commissioner of Works, gained an unexpected immortality by giving the name of 'Big Ben' to the great clock over the Houses of Parliament."

Wynford Vaughan-Thomas 1985

Benjamin Hall was elected MP for the Monmouth Boroughs in 1831 when he defeated the Marquis of Worcester by 168 votes to 149 votes. In the following year he beat the Marquis again by 393 votes to 355 when it appears the number of persons entitled to vote had more than doubled. He remained MP for the constituency until 1837, when he was elected to represent the London Borough of Marlyebone and continued as MP until his elevation to the peerage as Lord Llanover in 1859.

It was Benjamin Hall who laid the foundations of the future London County Council in 1855 with his Bill for the setting up of the Metropolitan Board of Works. It was later described as "the most important single measure passed for the government of London (which) for the first time introduced an ordered system."

In 1838 following the Coronation of Queen Victoria, Benjamin was made baronet and in 1854 he became a Privy Councillor. At this time he was President of the Board of Health and the next year he was appointed Commissioner of Works. During his term in office he transformed Battersea Park, London and was involved in the rebuilding of the Palace of Westminster, alternatively known as the House of Commons, which had been burnt down in 1834.

St Katherine's Lodge, which stood at the angle between Chester Road and the Broad Walk in Regent's Park was built by Sir Benjamin's orders, copied from a lodge at Llanover Park and roofed with tiles from his estate at Abercarn. Unfortunately the buiding was hit by a bomb during the Second World War.

A drinking fountain near Palace Gate in Kensington Gardens bears a plaque with the following inscription:

> This drinking fountain, erected in 1951, marks the site of an ancient spring which in 1856 was named St Govor's Well, after the patron saint of Llanover, by Sir Benjamin Hall, 1st Commissioner of Works, 1855-58. Created Lord Llanover in 1859.

Sir Benjamin took the name from the well of St Govor in the grounds of Llanover Park.

Benjamin Hall was responsible for many important reforms in the local government of London. As Commissioner of Public Works he planned London's water supply and also laid pipes to feed fountains - 'so that the poor would not need to quench their thirst at the gin-shops'. He was also instrumental in arranging for a huge bell to be cast and installed in the clock tower of the new Houses of Parliament.

The name 'Big Ben' was given to the deep sounding bell in the 320ft clock tower of the House of Commons to commemorate Benjamin Hall's association with the rebuilding of the Houses of Parliament

In the Illustrated London News of 6th March 1856 is an account of the arrival of the first bell (it was later recast). The account ends: "All Bells, we believe, are christened before they begin to toll, and on this occasion it is proposed to call our King of Bells, 'Big Ben' in honour of Sir Benjamin Hall, the President of the Board of Works, during whose tenure it was cast."

The bell was first cast on 6 August 1856 at Warner's of Norton, near Stockton-on-Tees and at 16 tons 11 cwts it was the biggest ever made in Britain. When completed it was transported by rail to West Hartlepool, to be taken by ship to London. But there were a few problems: it was dropped on to the deck of the ship causing structural damage and then nearly lost at sea in a storm.

When the bell at last arrived in London it was placed on a specially constructed carriage and pulled across Westminster bridge by sixteen white horses. It was then hung on a gallows in New Palace Yard and tested each day throughout 1857.

One hot summer afternoon in 1857, Parliament had a special sitting to decide on a suitable name for the bell, which had been called all kinds of names by various people. Many speeches were delivered and suggestions made. Then Sir Benjamin Hall rose to deliver the greatest oration of the day. Proposing the name of St Stephen he expounded his theme with high-sounding phrases at great length. As he was sinking back into his seat, mopping his brow with a large silk handkerchief, a waggish member, not waiting to catch the Speaker's eye, shouted "Why not call it BIG BEN and have done with it?" The House simply rocked with laughter and Big Ben it became thereafter.

A year later the bell was found to be cracked and it was then taken down to be re-cast. It was broken up in the Palace Yard and carted in small pieces to Whitechapel. The metal was melted in three furnaces, heated by wood fires and the amount increased to over 17 tons. The re-casting took place on April 10th, 1858. It took 20 minutes to fill the mould with molten metal and as many days for it to cool down.

The casting was judged to be almost perfect and close to the specified weight of 13 tons 10 cwt 3qtrs and 15 lbs. It was just the intended note of E. It was tested in various ways and the *Illustrated London News* of May 9th, 1858, stated, "The upper parts of this new bell are as sound as at the very bottom."

Mounted on a trolley drawn by sixteen gaily be-ribboned horses the bell was taken to Westminster with admiring crowds lining the route over London Bridge, along Borough Road and across Westminster Bridge. George Mears who had undertaken the re-casting wanted the bell to be named "Victoria" but the name Big Ben had caught the popular fancy and so it remained.

As the trolley rolled slowly towards Westminster the great bell gleamed in the sunshine, being coated with some sort of varnish which enhanced its general appearance.

The clock cost £40,000 and uses the double three legged gravity escapement invented by Edmund Beckett (afterwards Lord Grimthorpe), which became a standard for all really accurate tower clocks. The clock tower is 320 feet high and has four dials each 22 feet 6 inches in diameter with the minute hand 9 feet long. A light burns in this tower whenever Parliament is sitting.

Big Ben's first BBC broadcast was in the nature of a "surprise item" on December 31st, 1923. The Old Year was rung out by the Westminster Chimes and 1924 was ushered in by the deep, booming tones of the great hour bell. Letters of congratulation showered on the BBC during the next few days and Big Ben soon became a permanent feature. A microphone was installed in the belfry, above the hour bell, wired directly to Savoy Hill so that Big Ben could be brought into service, instantly and at any time by the pressing of a switch in the studio. The chimes became a daily feature on radio programmes and, in addition, were used to herald items of special importance.

Sir Benjamin Hall was raised to the peerage in 1859 and appointed Lord Lieutenant of Monmouthshire in November 1861 in succession to Capel Hanbury Leigh of Pontypool Park, who had died in September of that year.

Lord Llanover in uniform as
Lord Lieutenant of Monmouthshire, 1865

Although a very successful politician, Benjamin was essentially a countryman at heart and he liked nothing better than being with his horses and dogs. He was a first class horseman and also a good marksman who stalked Scottish moors as the opportunity arose. He remained a first-class shot even after losing an eye in a shooting accident in 1848. The family also had an extensive sporting estate at Abercarn which had been given to them by Richard Crawshay in 1808.

In November 1866, Benjamin began to suffer from an abscess which formed on the jaw where he had been 'kicked' by a new gun. He had been given the gun by Ifor Herbert, and when he fired it off it bruised his cheek. This happened twice but the injury was so slight that little notice was taken of it until the abscess formed.

In December his surgeon, Sir William Fergusson burnt out the abscess with caustic, deciding not to use a knife on the account of the loss of blood. Benjamin suffered agonies and morphine had to be administered three times before it took effect.

At this time Benjamin was in London and he longed to return to Llanover, but he was too weak to be moved. Sadly, on 27 April 1867, Lady Llanover wrote to her friend Betha Jones: "All is over. The light of my life is gone - He died at half past three this morning after fearful sufferings - but his last half-hour was peaceful, death like a child. I am very miserable. I *ought* to be more thankful for *him*."

The remains of Lord Llanover were taken to Llanover and the funeral was carried out in accordance with his written instructions:

> *"My funeral is to be as simple and inexpensive as possible. My remains are to be borne by such of my tenants and employees as shall be chosen for that purpose, and such people as shall express a desire to carry them. Pall-bearers to be chosen from among the tenants and overseers, and no crepe hatbands or scarves to be worn by anyone. No hired carriages, no mutes, no pompous military display. Welsh hymns are to be sung."*

On the day of the funeral, tenants gathered in the library and prayed in Nonconformist fashion, above his coffin, after which it was taken into the hall, where the Rev. R. J. Evans, Vicar of Llanover, prayed in Welsh and English. The Llanover choir sang the Welsh dirge *Gorffennwyd* (It is finished) as the remains were carried over the threshold, and Welsh hymns were sung as the procession made its way to the church, the entire three-quarters of a mile of roadway being strewn with myrtle and evergreens.

Present at the service were several clergymen: the Rev Charles Ranken Hall, the Rev A. J. Ram, the Rev David Howell, Vicar of St John's Cardiff; the Rev David Charles, Calvinistic Methodist Minister of the Welsh church at Abercarn and the Rev Robert Thomas, the Independent Minister of Llanover.

Other friends present included John Johnes of Dolaucothi and Henry Freshfield (Lord Llanover's executors) and Col. Morgan Clifford, the Deputy Lord-Lieutenant of Monmouthshire. There was an impressive train of family mourners, including Halls, Herberts, Berringtons, Waddingtons, de Bunsens and Captain Ross. In addition there was a long procession of servants and tenants.All the women wore black Welsh hats, white caps and aprons and black shawls.

Lord Llanover's will was simple and direct. He left everything to "my dear wife, who knows and shares my wishes". During the next thirty years Lady Llanover did her utmost to carry out his wishes just like Queen Victoria carried out those of the Prince Consort, though she did not shut herself away from the world. Instead, she found refuge in her work for Wales and for others, but the anniversaries of Lord Llanover's birthday or death were never forgotten.

The Children of Lord and Lady Llanover

Augusta and Benjamin had two sons and one daughter. Sadly, both the sons had short lives. Benjamin Craddock Hall died in June 1836 at the age of five. He was buried in Kensal Green Cemetery, London and the grave was planted with evergreens in the Welsh tradition, with a stone cross "of the ancient British form' to mark the head. For the rest of her life, when in London, Augusta never failed to visit the grave with fresh flowers.

Benjamin Hanbury Stewart Hall died on 11th February1845 , just eight days before his nineteenth birthday. He was buried in the family vault at Llanover churchyard.

In 1846, the Hon Augusta Charlotte Elizabeth Hall, married Arthur Jones a Squire of Llanarth who under a royal seal assumed the surname of Herbert in 1848. They lived at Llanarth Court until 1895 when on the death of her husband, Augusta returned to live with her mother at Llanover House, who passed away the following year at the age of 94.

Like her mother, Augusta was a remarkable linguist being a fluent conversationalist in English, Welsh, German, French and Italian. Two of her sons inherited this talent to a remarkable degree, for General Sir Ifor Herbert was credited with being one of the most accomplished linguists in the House of Commons while Sir Arthur Herbert also possessed notabley similar attributes.

7

Llanover Church

"The church of Llanover stands in a romantic position, on the banks of the Usk, about half a mile from the house (Llanover House); it is a handsome gothic ediface, consisting of a high embattled tower of hewn stone, a nave and chancel, and by the care of Mr Waddington is kept in an extraordinary state of order and neatness."

William Coxe 1801

L lanover Church (SO 318094) is situated near the River Usk on the east side of Llanover Park. To reach it by car, drive in an easterly direction down a narrow lane leading off the A4042, near Porth Mawr. Turn right at a T-junction to shortly arrive at a parking area near the lych gate.

The dedication is to St Bartholomew but there is a tradition that the first church here was founded by St Gover who studied at the monastic community of St Serio at Penmon, Anglesey. On completing his religious education, it would seem that he travelled down to Gwent with his fellow monk St Ffwyst who gave his name to Llanfoist, where the church bears the anglicised dedication to St Faith. The name Gover is preserved in Llanover Park with the name of a spring - Ffynnon Over - the well of Gover.

Llanover used to be the mother church of Trevethin, Pontypool (separated in 1843), Mamhilad (separated in 1855) and Capel Newydd (demolished 1893). The register of baptisms and burials dates from 1661, marriages from 1754 and Vicars of the church are listed from 1535.

The massive embattled tower of Llanover Church has been constructed in three stages and it contains five bells. An interesting feature is the sundial about three-quarters of the way up from the ground.

When you enter the south porch which was rebuilt in 1750 lift up the mat and pause to examine the stone slab, much worn by centuries of passing feet. It bears a cross incised in a circle and there is a local belief that it once covered the grave of St Gover. However, experts have dated the stone to the 14th century.

Surrounding the font is a large enclosed panelled area, reconstructed from sections of two oak pews belonging to the Prichard family of Llanover. The back of the pew is carved with a dragon's head, holding in its mouth a sinister hand couped at the wrist. A brass plate bearing an English inscription in Roman capitals commemorates two brothers of that family, William and Matthew:

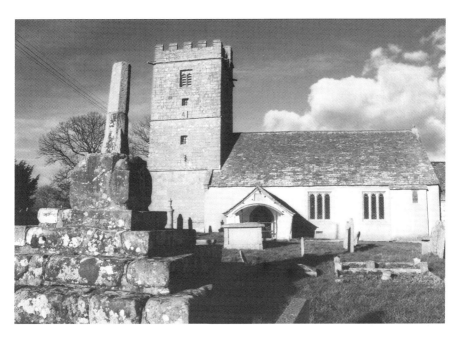

St Bartholomew's Church Llanover and Churchyard Cross

Below the inner door of the church porch is a long narrow slab and carved on it is a simple cross. There is a local tradition that this stone once covered the grave of St Gover.

The top two-thirds of the brass is occupied by a central shield-of-arms, with mantling, helmet and crest, flanked by two male figures in armour, both standing with hands placed together in prayer. They wear breast-plates, ridged down the front, with laminated plates covering shoulders and arms. Hinged to the skirt of the breast-plate are two laminated tassets, strapped down over voluminous trunk-hose, covering the thighs to the knees; the rivets of the armour are carefully delineated, and projecting from beneath the tassets, shoulder pieces and breast -plate are the scalloped edges of the linings. The figures are bare-headed and each wears a sword.

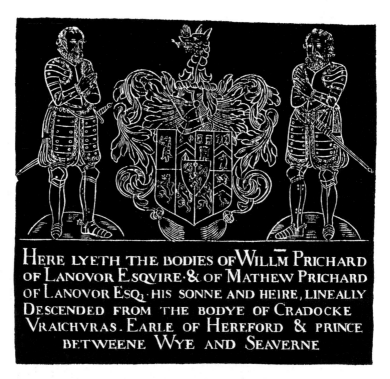

HERE LYETH THE BODIES OF WILLM PRICHARD OF LANOVOR ESQVIRE·& OF MATHEW PRICHARD OF LANOVOR ESQ · HIS SONNE AND HEIRE, LINEALLY DESCENDED FROM THE BODYE OF CRADOCKE VRAICHVRAS. EARLE OF HEREFORD & PRINCE BETWEENE WYE AND SEAVERNE

The Squire's pew bears a brass plate to the memory of Matthew Prichard, who claimed to be a direct descendant of Caradoc Freichfras, a Welsh Prince. The crest of the Prichard family is carved on the back of the pew; a wyverne's head, holding in the mouth a hand couped at the wrist, with an inscription: 'The armes of M.P. of Llanover, Esquier.' This ancient family resided at Cwrt Porth-hir (now a farmhouse), and were succeeded by the Rumseys.

Matthew Prichard was High Sheriff of Monmouthshire in 1596, and died in 1610, to which date the brass probably belongs. The arms represented appear to belong to William, as his wife belonged to the Herbert family, and the escutcheon-of-pretence was the appropriate way of quartering the arms of a wife. The elaborate arms illustrate the tendency of Welsh gentry of the day to include the arms attributed to all the ancestors from whom they claimed descent.

At the back of the same pew is a dexter hand grasping a sword, with an inscription: 'The armes of Water Rumsey of Llannover, Esquier, Linealie descended from the Bodie of Water Rumsey, Knight, Lord Baronet of the Lordshippe and Town of Rumsey, in Hampshire.'

Walter Rumsey was born in Llanover in 1584. He was a noted lawyer, often called the Picklock of the Law because of his large practice. In 1631 he was made a judge, but sixteen years later, having taken an active part on the side of Charles I during the Civil War, he was dismissed from office by order of Parliament. He was buried in Llanover Church in 1660, just after the Restoration had restored him to high office.

The coat of arms, which is painted in oils directly onto the back wall of the church, dates back to between 1816 and 1837 and relates to either George IV or William IV. The work was carried out during the time of Lady Llanover, but prior to its discovery in 1938, the coat of arms had been painted over. Restoration of this unique coat of arms to its former glory was carried out a few years ago by conservator, Ruth Davies of Tiverton, Devon, at a cost of £7,000. The costs were covered by grants from Cadw, the Diocesan Churches Fund and Gwent County Council's Welsh Churches Fund.

Epitaph of Walter Cecil

'Here under lyeth ye Body
of Walter Cecil: Esq. who depart
ed this Life ye 18. day of April,
Anno Dom. 1754. Aged 69 years.'

The shield of arms marks his relationship to the Earls of Exeter and Salisbury. Their common ancestor, Robert Sitsylt or Cecil, assisted Robert Fitzhamon in the conquest of Glamorgan. His descendant Richard, lord of Alt yr ynys, left two sons, Philip and David who resided at Stamford in Lincolnshire, and ancestor of the Earls of Salisbury and Exeter. Philip, the eldest son, was the owner of Allt yr ynys, and his descendants had large possessions in Herefordshire and Monmouthshire. Walter, interred here at Llanover, was the last of this family who possessed Ty Uchaf.

The Coat of Arms and the motto of the Llanover family
which reads 'Ni ddaw da o hir arofin'

The chancel has simple altar rails dated 1700 and a beautifully coloured modern east window showing Christ with a bishop and an apostle.

A large memorial slab commemorates the Waddington family and two hatchments, one for Benjamin Waddington (d.1828) and the other for Lord Llanover (d.1867).

Another memorial of interest is one to John Jones 'domestic harper to Sir Be. Hall Bart' and the inscription which is in Welsh, also records that he had 'played the harp with applause before Queen Victoria.'

Lady Llanover regularly attended afternoon services at Llanover Church, being driven there by her liveried coachman. As she walked in through the door, everyone in the church stood up and she was of course the first person to leave the building after the service.

At Christmas time she gave prizes to Sunday School scholars. These were often red scarfs made at Gwenffrwd the local woollen factor that she had established.

Llanover Church was always crowded for the Plygain service and it must have been quite a sight to see the congregation converging on the church on a frosty Christmas morning, with everyone carrying a lighted and decorated candle. The Plygain is a carol service and the name comes from a Latin word meaning 'cock-crow' or 'dawn' and the service originally followed the Midnight Mass, but gradually was held later, until 6 am became the accepted hour.

> *"I lit my decorated candle and sallied out into the darkness with the others, the path down to the church was quite illuminated by the many candles... The choir sang a few pieces and the Canon preached. After the service was over, we took up our candles, and some of us carried them up to the house still alight.."*

> Margaret Davies 1861

The vicars of Llanover between 1831 and the death of Lady Llanover in 1896, were: John Evans (d.1859); William Jones (resigned 1862 to go to Llandwnog, Caernarvonshire); Joshua Evans (resigned 1891 on being appointed to St James's Pontypool); and Evan Davies.

> *"The church is old looking and small and consequently looked pretty full. All the servants belonging to the Hall were there. High hats, and a few ladies besides her Ladyship also wore one."*

> Margaret Davis 1861

This stone depicting a harp marks the grave of John Jones the Llanover family harpist who died in December 1844 at the age of only forty-four. The inscription in Welsh traces his 'musical descent' from the famous Welsh harpists of the seventeenth century:

> 'Here lies John Jones, domestic harper to Sir B. Hall, of Llanover, Bart., and formerly of Dolgellau, in Merioneth, who died December 12th, 1844, aged 44. He excelled on the triple harp, and gained the silver harp at the Brecon Eisteddfod of 1826; and performed on the harp with applause before Her Majesty Queen Victoria, at the royal palace in 1843. He was a pupil of Richard Roberts, of Caernarvon; whose tutor was William Williams, of Penmorfa; whose tutor was John Parry of Ruabon, the original of Gray's Bard; whose tutor was Robert Parry, of Llanllyfni, in Arfon, who derived his art from the ancient harpers of Wales.'

John Jones's successor was his pupil Thomas Gruffydd who came from Llangynidr and was for many years recognised as the greates harpist of his day.

Churchyard Cross, Llanover

This suspension bridge (no public access) used to be known locally as 'Mr Pym's Bridge.' A previous one, constructed of wood was built for the father of Francis Pym, once the Foreign Secretary in Mrs Thatcher's Government. Francis spent his childhood at Penpergwm Lodge, near Abergavenny, when his father was land agent for the Llanover Estate.

"The Boathouse quite overhangs the river. Here old Morgan Jones lived. His son John was the leader of her Ladyship's choir, and his daughter Margaret was one of the singers."

8
The Death of Lady Llanover

Lady Llanover died on Friday 17 January 1896 at the age of 94. She had outlived practically all her friends and was buried the following Thursday. A surviving friend was Betha Jones, the daughter of Judge John Johnes of Dolau Cothi. She wrote in a letter, after the funeral: 'no-one can replace the dear old Friend in her old home - but it is best she should be at peace, and at the age of 94, she died as she had lived, a worker.'

> *"We very much regret to announce the death of Lady Llanover, which took place somewhat suddenly at her residence at Llanover on Friday afternoon, last at the advanced age of 95 years.*
>
> *Down to a few minutes before her dissolution her ladyship bore not the slightest indication that there was anything the matter with her. She had spent the day in bed, and at three o' clock Miss Price served her with luncheon. Suddenly it became apparent that her ladyship had grown unconscious. Mrs Evans, her maid, was called and the state of unconsciousness continued, and the Rev John Prys was sent for. He quickly came, but only in time to see the venerable lady pass away."*

Pontypool Free Press

The Hon Mrs Herbert, of Llanarth, her ladyship's only surviving daughter, arrived on Saturday at noon with her three sons: Colonel Ivor Herbert of the Grenadier Guards; Major Bleddyn Herbert of the 17th Lancers and Mr Arthur Herbert of the Diplomatic Service.

LANOVER CHURCH

The Funeral

"It was a heavy and oppressive day. The morning dawned with every indication of a storm, but the rain-clouds rolled away to be succeeded by a thick overhanging mist that enwrapped the country as in a shroud. The midday trains were heavily laden with tenants who were assembling from far and near to pay their last tribute of respect to Lady Llanover.

For many hours the roads leading from Abergavenny, Penpergwm, Nantyderry and Pontypool towards Llanover were traversed by a continuous stream of mourners on foot, on horseback, and in vehicles, all without exception attired in the deepest of black.

Although the funeral was in a sense a private one, the family had extended a ready permission to tenants who desired to attend, and many hundreds availed themselves of that permission accordingly.

Shortly after 1 o' clock the remains were brought from the bedroom and placed on a bier in the large central hall to the left of the principal entrance. The body lay in a coffin of oak, protected by a shell of lead, the whole being encased in Llanover oak with heavy brass trimmings, the breastplate bearing the inscription:-

LADY LLANOVER
Born 21st March, 1802
Died 17th January, 1896
Aged 95 years
South Wales Daily News

After Lady Llanover's death in January 1896 her daughter, the Hon Mrs Herbert, who had long since embraced her late husband's faith, came to reside at Llanover Park and Roman Catholic priests henceforth constantly visited the house. When the first priest came to stay and say mass at Llanover, he was asked next morning at breakfast, according to the polite old custom, how he had passed the night, with the hope that he had slept soundly.

"Oh well to be quite honest," came the unexpected reply, "I could not get a wink of sleep all night long. Whenever I was on the point of dropping asleep, a large bee came at me and buzzed angrily in my ear. Several times I got out of bed and pursued this bee to the window, but there it always vanished, only to return as soon as my head touched the pillow. And this trouble continued until it was broad daylight."

The company at the table exchanged meaning glances. Was not the late Lady Llanover's bardic name 'Gwenynen Gwent' (which might be extended to mean the Queen Bee of South Wales)? She had often proclaimed herself to be 'a Protestant Trinitarian Christian'. Was then, this elusive bee her indignant spirit risen to protest against the presence of a Roman Catholic priest in Protestant Llanover?

The Tomb of Lord and Lady Llanover

"They lie side by side in a magnificent melancholy mausoleum in Llanover Churchyard, covered all over with Cymric texts and symbols, and surmounted by the arms the couple had devised for themselves upon Benjamin's elevation to the peerage, supported by a dragon and a horned goat."

Jan Morris 1984

Designed by Lord Llanover himself, this tomb must surely be the largest in Gwent. It bears many inscriptions in Welsh and English and a large coat of arms. The tomb was constructed by Mr W. Meredyth Thomas and erected by local workmen under his personal direction.

Coat of Arms of Lord and Lady Llanover
on the eastern end of their magnificent tomb

Access to the interior of the tomb is through a door at the western end of the tomb

Over the entrance to the tomb are the words in Welsh:

"I know that my Redeemer liveth," and underneath the words of the Psalmist, "Ac yn Awr, beth a ddisgwyliaf, O Argwydd? Fy nghobaith sydd ynot ti." - "And now, Lord what is my hope? Truly my hope is even in Thee."

Other Welsh and English inscriptions, together with elaborate carvings symbolic of the Welsh sympathies of the family, embelish the edges and panels.

When Lady Llanover's daughter died, she was interred in the family tomb to rest alongside the remains of her parents, her brother Mr Hanbury Hall and her youngest son Stephen Herbert.

Mrs Augusta Charlotte Elizabeth Herbert of Llanover House and of Ty Uchaf, Llanover and of Abercarn House and of 9 Great Stanhope Street, Mayfair, London, died on November 3rd 1912 aged 89. She left estate of the gross value of £92,861 13s 9d.

She was born at Abercarn House where her parents lived for a short time before the erection of Llanover Hall in 1824. In 1846 she married John Jones of Llanarth Court. Two years later their surname was changed to Herbert. They had four sons and a daughter:

Sir Ivor Herbert of Llanarth Court, Sir Arthur Herbert of Coldbrook House, Colonel Edward Bleiddian Herbert of Trebencyn and the Hon Mrs Maxwell.

9
Lord Treowen

Ivor John Caradoc Herbert was born in 1851, being the eldest son of Mr J.A.E. Herbert D.L., J.P., of Llanarth Court and the Hon Augusta Charlotte Herbert, only daughter of the first Baron Llanover. One of his ancestors was Sir Richard Herbert of Coldbrook and another direct ancestor was Sir Philip Jones of Treowen.

He commenced his military career with the Grenadier Guards which he joined as a subaltern in 1870 at the age of 19 and was appointed captain in 1874. He fought as a major with the Brigade of Guards in the Egyptian Campaign of 1882 and again with the Guards' Camel Corps in the Nile Expedition of 1884-5. He was in the field again in the South African War.

Ivor was an accomplished linguist, speaking several languages fluently and his honours included the C.B., the C.M.G., the Legion of Honour, the Order of the Crown of Italy, the Second Class Medjidie and the German Order of the Red Eagle.

Lieutenant Herbert as he was then married in 1873 Albertina the younger daughter of Lord Londesborough. Their only son was Captain Elidyr Herbert of the Monmouthshire Squadron of the Royal Gloucestershire hussars who was killed in action in Palestine in 1917.

From 1886 till 1890, Sir Ivor Herbert, as he was then, was Military Attache at St Petersburg and for the five following years he commanded the Militia of Canada.

He retired in 1908 with the rank of Major-General and two years later he entered Parliament for the old South Monmouthshire Division. He held his seat until 1917, when he was created Lord Treowen of Treowen and Llanarth. On the death of Lord Tredegar of Balaclava fame, he was appointed Lord Lieutenant of Monmouthshire.

In 1925 Lord Treowen built the model village of Tre Elidyr (Elidyr's Town) at Llanover, named in memory of his only son Elidyr. The architect was Alfred Powell, who was an associate of Ernest Gimson and the Barnsleys.

Lord Treowen died at the age of 82, on 19th October 1933 at Llanarth Court after a serious illness. He was buried at Llanarth Parish Churchyard following requiem mass in the private chapel at Llanarth Court. With his death passed away the sole remaining grandchild of Augusta, Lady Llanover.

Lord Treowen (1851-1933),
Grandson of Lord and Lady Llanover

10
Llanarth Court

" We are all so used now to the name of Herbert of Llanarth, that few of us are left to recall the fact that the real name of this ancient family is the fine old patronymic of Jones."

Herbert Vaughan 1926

Lanarth Court stands on a ridge facing approximately north and south, within a fine terrace on both sides. It was built in 1790 on the site of a much older house called Hendre Obaith ('the old home of hope'). This was an Elizabethan mansion, with terraced gardens, at the bottom of which flows the Clawr brook. At the end of the sixteenth century, Philip Jones of Treowen came to live at Hendre Obaith. He had made a large fortune in London and was Member of Parliament for the Monmouth Borough from 1588 to 1593. In particular he is remembered for building a town hall and market-house in Monmouth and in his will he left 200 marks to build a similar market-house in Abergavenny. It was during the latter years of his life that he resided at Hendre Obaith and when he died there in 1603, he was buried in Llanarth Church.

It was John Jones (of Llanarth, Treowen and Wonastow), who demolished the old house and built the present mansion which stands in a 240 acre park, laid out in 1792 by Samuel Lapidge in the style of Capability Brown.

The cellars are the only remaining portion of the ancient building, the walls of which are of remarkable thickness. There are long narrow underground passages, one of which goes to the grounds through a tiny door to a door marked with a red cross, which opens to reveal a stone altar in a tiny cell-like apartment. This was the secret chapel of the Roman Catholic family in the days when to perform the service of Mass was high treason.

In the grounds is a Catholic Chapel (GR 381105), built in 1780 and from that time a priest was maintained by the family. The Herbert family of Llanarth adhered to the Roman Catholic church during the centuries when the penal laws against 'Papists' were in force. In 1750 the family built this chapel of Our Lady and St Michael. It is simple in form with the nave and apse separated by two slender columns.

In the apse are two fine modern windows, depicting St Francis and St Bernard, set there in memory of Lord Treowen (d.1933) and Bernard Herbert. The nave is lighted by a series of windows containing painted Flemish or German 17th century glass which was installed when the chapel was first built.

Llanarth Court

The Lodge, Llanarth Court

Llanarth Court was remodelled by W and E Habersham in 1851 and today it is an independent hospital, owned and managed by Partnership in Care Limited. A specialised assessment and treatment service is provided for mentally disordered adults 'with a variety of challenging behaviours'. Accommodation is provided in five secure units with a total of 71 beds and an open unit of 10 beds.

The Jones family lived at Treowen, an early 17th century manor house, before they moved to Llanarth. It has been claimed that this is the tallest house in Monmouthshire.

11
Llanarth Church

The parish church, dedicated to St Teilo was restored in the nineteenth century by Sir Thomas Phillips, who was Mayor of Newport at the time of the Chartists' riots. A brass tablet at the west end of the Church describes his virtues. His interest in this church was due to his brother-in-law Canon W. Price being the vicar from 1828 to 1878.

Major restoration work was carried out between 1989 and 1991, which involved complete re-roofing, replacement of weathered stonework around the windows and repairs to the tower.

St Teilo's Church, Llanarth

Inside the church, on the north wall is a large memorial stone extolling the virtues of Elizabeth Jones (d.1787) the wife of William Jones of Clytha (fourth son of John Jones of Llanarth Court). She is buried in the churchyard. The following lines are just part of the long description of her virtues:

Her Goodness and her Worth
were so eminently conspicuous, that most finished monumental eulogy
would vainly endeavour to display them.
Yet as she always modestly shrunk from observation,
and studiously strove to conceal her various Endowments,
Justice to her memory requires
that some, tho' a very imperfect sketch of her character be here
attempted:
She was blest with every hereditary Virtue
of the Most illustrious House of Cavendish:
meek, humble, patient,
generous, friendly, noble;
Happily adorn'd with a most extensive Genius,
her Knowledge was vast and uncommon;
in Poetry, Music, Botany, and all the polite Arts,
She excelled;
as her Manuscripts abundantly testify;
To enumerate her vitues was impossible;
She was, in short,
Purity and Innocence itself:
for if ever those Virues were personified,
they were in her.
An utter Stranger to every species of Detraction,
She never spoke of her neighbour, but with praise and
commendation.
With a Heart ever bleeding at the Distress of others,
the great business and delight of her Life was
'To do good, and to distribute.'
Being too good to continue any longer in this World.

A flat stone within low rails is inscribed:

> Here lyeth the body of
> John Arthur Herbert
> Of Llanarth Court Esq.,
> Who died on the 18th Aug
> 1895, aged 76 years
> RIP

There is a shield of Herbert and around the edge of the stone is written:
My soul hath waited on his word, My soul hath hoped in the Lord, For with the Lord there is mercy, And with him is plenteous redemption.

A stone carved with a cross and the arms of the Herbert family marks the grave of Sir John Arthur Herbert, who died in Calcutta in 1943 when Governor of Bengal.

WALKS IN LLANOVER COUNTRY

The maps required for these walks are the Ordnance Survey Explorer 13 and 152. Choose suitable footwear and be prepared for occasional muddy paths, particularly after a period of rain. If you intend to lead a party around an unfamiliar walk, particularly one which crosses farmland, it is always advisable to check the route beforehand so that you can be sure of taking your group the correct way, and always respect the Country Code.

WALK ONE
The Llanover Circuit

4 miles 6.4 kilometres

"Surely no more delectable countryside could be imagined. Against a background of mountains, the colours of which change from moment to moment like shot silk, set amongst the noblest trees in the county, and threaded by one of the fairest reaches of the Usk, this green land called for men's best efforts into converting it into a site for a village."

Fred Hando 1958

START: Layby on the west side of the A4042 (G.R. 306093)

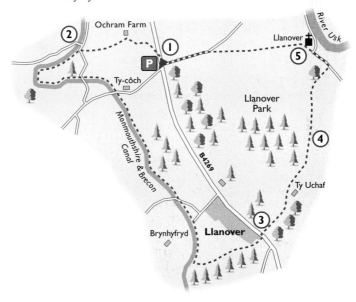

1. From the north end of the layby follow a lane uphill past Ochram Mill. On reaching Ochram Farm, bear left and go over a stile. Turn right beside a hedge and continue through a field. Keep straight on at the end of the hedge to reach a stile and go up to the towpath of the Monmouthshire & Brecon Canal (constructed in 1797-1812).

2. Turn left along the towpath and follow it for 1 ½ miles. On passing under Bridge 79 go over a stile and head down the right side of a field to reach a hunting gate. Continue with a hedge on your right and shortly bear slightly right to descend beside a fence with part of the old village of Llanover below you now on the right. The track leads down into a small parking area near the Post Office.

3. Cross the A4042 with care, go through the main entrance to Llanover Park and walk down the tree lined drive. (A sign indicates that this is a private road, but there is a right of way for walkers). Take the second turning on the left to follow the tarmac lane through Llanover Park. Ty Uchaf, the birthplace of Lady Llanover, will be seen across to the right. Take the next turning on the left, cross a cattle grid and go immediately right along a waymarked path leading through the trees. Ignore other paths to the left, but shortly on the left you will get a glimpse of the old stable block of the now demolished Llanover House. This building is on private land so do not stray off the path. Keep straight on at the next junction to shortly emerge from the trees at a stile.

4. Cross the field bearing slightly left as indicated by the waymark and shortly the tower of Llanover Church will be seen. Head directly towards it to reach a stile in the corner of the field. The long white building on the left is Hen Bersondy (Old Parsonage). After crossing the stile keep straight on with a fence on your right to reach a stile beside a gate. Turn left along the road to reach Llanover Church.

5. After visiting the church go over a stile in the top right corner of the churchyard and keep straight on with a hedge on your right. After about ¼ mile look out for a stile beside a gate on the right. After crossing it, keep straight on with the hedge now on your left. There are good views from here of Blorenge, Sugar Loaf, Ysgyryd Fach and Ysgyryd Fawr. Go over a stile and turn left along a road to shortly pass Cwrt Porth-hir farmhouse on the left. Follow the lane up to the main road and on the left will be seen the old Porth Mawr gatehouse (private). Turn right along the pavement beside the A4042 and cross it with care to reach your starting point in the layby.

WALK TWO
Beside the Usk

A pleasant walk in delightful countryside at any time of the year.

4 miles 6. kilometres

START: From a small layby just short of Pant-y-Goitre bridge
(G.R. 348088). Please do not obstruct the gateway
with your car as requested by the sign.

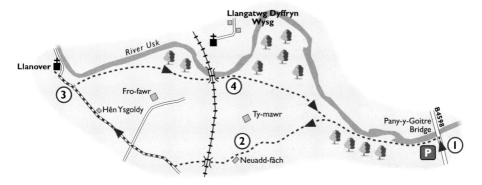

1. Walk up the road a short way and go over a stile on the left just before the bridge. Follow a path through the field with the River Usk on your right. In due course the parkland narrows and a stile is reached. Continue with the path now much narrower, passing above a ditch. Go right over a footbridge spanning a stream and continue through the riverside field. Shortly bear left to pass between a fence and a ruined building. Then go left through a small wooden gate to enter a fenced compound and go through another gate directly opposite. Go over a stile and continue with a fence on your left, following the edge of the field. After about ¼ mile a footbridge over a stream is reached. Shortly afterwards go over a stile and cross a small field to reach another stile.

2. Cross the next field to pass to the right of a barn and farmhouse. Cross the farm drive and continue with a fence/hedge on the left to reach a stile below a railway embankment. Ascend a steep flight of steps to reach the railway line (main line from Newport to Abergavenny and Hereford). Obey the sign which tells you to 'Stop, Look, Listen. Beware of Trains'. Go straight across the railway track and descend a flight of steps on the other side to go over a stile. Continue straight across the next field, passing to the

left of two oak trees to cross a cattle grid and turn right along a tarmac road. Continue along the road keeping straight on at a crossroads and the tower of Llanover Church will shortly come into view. If you wish to visit the church continue along the road. Otherwise turn right over a stile signposted 'Pant y Goitre Bridge'.

3. Follow the left edge of the field and soon you will be overlooking the river Usk. At the end of the field go over a stile on the left and continue with the path now descending to river level. Continue through the field keeping to the right. Go through a gate and then walk on beside the river to pass beneath a railway viaduct. Pass through a gate and continue along the left side of the field. Pause for a moment to look across the river at St Catwg's Church at Llangattock-nigh-Usk. This village is also known as The Bryn (the bank) and it was once situated much closer to the river which once flowed close to the churchyard wall but is now much further south of the church.

4. Continue along the right hand side of the field with the river now making a wide bend around to the left. Follow a broad rutted track to pass under some electricity wires. When the track divides, keep straight on to reach a stile. Ahead now will be seen the ruined building you passed earlier. The path leads you to the right hand side of the field passing to the right of a metal barn and the ruined building. Here you rejoin your outward route which is followed back to the start.

Pant-y-Goitre Bridge

WALK THREE
To the Goose and Cuckoo Inn

7.5 miles 12 kilometres

START: Foxhunter car park on the road between the B4246
leading to Abergavenny and Llanelen (G.R. 263107).

*This car park is named after Lt. Col. Harry Llewelyn's famous international show
jumping horse. The grave of 'Foxhunter' with its descriptive memorial plaque lies
a short walk along a path leading from the north side of the car park.*

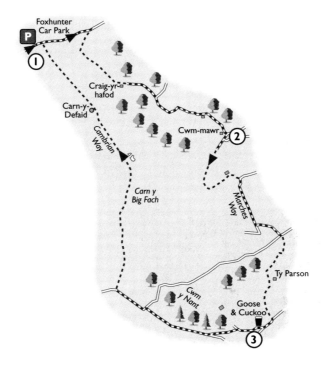

1. Commence the walk by heading north-east down the road from the car
park. After ½ mile leave the road by the Carn-y-gorfydd layby and join a
bridleway heading in a south west direction. Follow the path around a
cwm and join a metalled track at Craig-yr-hafod. There are fine views
across the Usk Valley with the peaks of Ysyryd Fawr and Graig Syyrddin
in the distance. Descend the lane and after a while the old manor house of
of Cwm-mawr with its very high gable end will be seen on the right.

2. Turn right up a very steep access road and at the entrance to Pentwyn turn sharp right onto a signed bridleway and ascend a woodland path. Contour around the head of a cwm and reach a lane just past Graig-y-Cwm Farm. Turn right along the access road to Yewtree Farm; take the right fork after 100 yards and ascend an ancient sunken lane. You are now following part of 'The Marches Way' which runs for 204 miles along the English/Welsh borderland from Cardiff to Chester. After ¼ mile take a distinct left fork and soon emerge onto the Blaenavon to Llanover lane. Go straight across and follow waymarked paths in a generally southerly direction for ½ mile to emerge onto a road just below the Goose and Cuckoo Inn.

Walkers are assured a warm welcome at this traditional country inn which is open every day except Monday. Here one can enjoy real ales and delicious home-cooked food. This is the only pub in the locality which survived the attentions of Lady Llanover, who turned the pubs on her estate into coffee houses!

The Goose and Cuckoo Inn

3. When you are ready to depart, head west up the lane and join a forestry track in the direction signed Cwmavon/Blaenavon. At an intersection of tracks continue on a forestry track ahead (not the waymarked bridleway) and rejoin the Blaenavon road. Head towards Blaenavon and soon the town comes into view, with Coity Mountain to the west.

4. Leave the road after ¼ mile, turning right at the footpath sign by a spring known as the 'Mountain Well'. Follow a well waymarked path across the moorland of Mynydd y Garn-fawr. passing the overgrown pools of Pwll Mawr and a large heap of stones which is a Bronze Age burial mound called Carn-y-Defaid. You are now walking part of the 'Cambrian Way'. This is a 274 mile high level route between Cardiff and Conwy. There is no official route and it is not waymarked. Make for the radio masts ahead to return to your starting point.

The Goose and Cuckoo Inn
This delightful little pub is very popular with walkers and it is owned and run by Michael and Carol Langley. The opening hours are:-
11.30am - 3pm and 7pm - 11pm on Tuesday, Wednesday and Thursday. 11.30am - 11pm on Friday and Saturday and 12pm- 10.30pm on Sunday. It is closed on Mondays but open all day on Bank Holidays. Real Ales are served and there is a large collection of malt whiskys. Children are welcome and one can enjoy traditional home cooking. Overnight camping with cooked breakfast is available. Also, Bed and Breakfast in one twin room with en suite bathroom @ £20 per person per night. Telephone: 01873 880277
gooseandcuckoo@lineone.net
www.avonhouse.freeuk.com/cuckoosnest/

WALK FOUR
The Canal, the Goose and the Holy Well

This walk takes in a section of the Monmouthshire & Brecon canal, the Goose and Cuckoo inn and the Holy Well under Mynydd Garn-wen. A variety of terrain, views and real ales. The maps are essential to follow paths across enclosed ground plus a compass for the open mountain.

Distance: 10 miles 16 kilometres

START: Penperlleni village car park,
6 miles south of Abergavenny on the A4042. (G.R.322046)

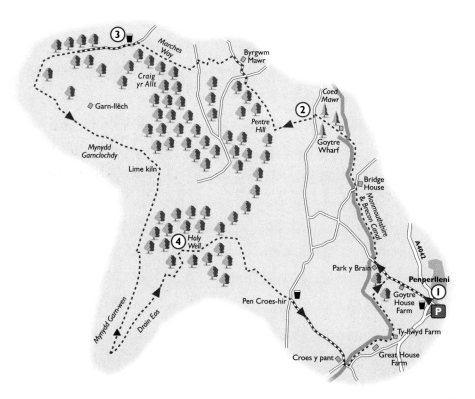

1. Cross the A4042 and walk up Park-y-brain lane to join the canal at Bridge 72. Walk for ¾ mile along the towpath to Goytre Wharf. The canal was completed between Gilwern and Brecon in 1800 and was initially used for agricultural purposes, carrying farm produce, lime and manure. Industrial products were only carried when the canal was extended southwards to Pontymoile in 1812 and connected with the Monmouthshire canal leading to Newport. The wharf has been developed into a fine recreational centre with a marina and boat hire facilities, shop, restaurant and canal interpretation centre. Turn right off the towpath, pass underneath the canal and walk up the access road.

Reconstruction of Goytre Wharf by Michael Blackmore

2. Cross the public highway and then ascend four fields via waymarked stiles and enter woodland. Turn right and follow the lower edge of the woodland, bearing right at a fork , and then right again to drop down to a lane. Bear left then right past Ty-Byrgwm cottage. Soon afterwards leave the lane turning left over a stile. Follow a waymarked path across four fields and into the lane by Coed-Robin cottage (take care to keep to the north side of the property, not taking the inviting looking stile into the grounds!). Head up across one more field, enter the Craig yr Allt woodland and turning half right join 'The Marches Way' long distance trail. The 'Goose and Cuckoo' is soon in sight where a warm welcome is assured to all walkers.

The Holy Well

Ffynnon Angoeron (very cold well), to use its Welsh name, is situated on the eastern side of a wooded cwm at SO 297052. It is constructed of stone and is supplied by a stream that has its source in the slope above.

When T.H. Thomas of Cardiff cleaned the well out in 1890, he found pins, a nail, a schoolboy's slate pencil, a few buttons and a copper gilt brooch. He accordingly decided that it had been used as a wishing well and claimed that in order for the wish to come true it had to be spoken silently (i.e thought) or the wish would be broken.

Francis Jones in his book *The Holy Wells of Wales*, published in 1954 states that the well was one of five Monmouthshire pin wells and was thus a holy well. The origin of this well is not known, but it can be surmised that it was once on the side of a track leading from Trevethin over Garn Wen, past the well, on to Pencroesoped and Llanover. This track was probably established in the Middle Ages when a chapel at Trevethin was annexed to Llanover Church.

Pins were used as offerings at British wells in Roman times and there is evidence of this in many parts of Britain. They represented offerings to the deity of the well for the favour that the person hoped to receive. The pins were often bent in order to exorcise the evil spirit supposed to afflict the person who dropped them.

At some wells the behaviour of the offering was believed to indicate whether or not the wish would be granted. For example at one particular well in Glamorgan, into which pins were thrown, if the pin became discoloured in the water, it was a sign that the wish would be granted.

All kinds of objects were left as offerings by pilgrims visiting holy wells in medieval times and also right through the centuries. Even today, people throw coins into 'wishing wells'. Any object left at a holy well should not be disturbed and certainly not stolen. It was once believed that any illness suffered by the giver would then be transferred to the thief.

3. Turn right up the lane after leaving the pub and fork left in the direction signed Cwmavon. Bear left through a gate into a wood and follow a sunken track lined with ancient beech trees. At an intersection go straight across following a rough, stoney track and pass through two metal gates to emerge onto the open mountain. At another intersection turn left and follow a well defined track along the summit ridge, southeast and then south, for two miles to reach the trig point on Mynydd Garn-wen (425m). There are fine views across the valley of the Usk, and to the Black Mountains and the Brecon Beacons; ahead you can see Newport and across the Bristol Channel to the Mendips and North Somerset coast. Just past the trig point descend from the ridge and double back north-east along a track. Pick up a fence line and where it turns right follow it downhill. This is a steep section and bracken can be a problem. Ignore a stile to the right, instead turning left and follow around the top of a wood and drop down into a wooded cwm.

4. Follow the waymarked path down to the Holy Well. This is a small, stone structure containing a murky pool. Its name suggests a reputation for healing powers and a place of pilgrimage in medieval times. When the path emerges from the woodland bear right across the stream and follow waymarked paths generally southeast across the fields to the Horseshoe Inn. Cross the road here and follow the lane for ½ mile to rejoin the canal at Croes-y-pant bridge. Turn northwards and in ½ mile leave the towpath, bearing off right through a wooden gate into Goytre Home Wood. This is owned and manageds by the Gwent Ornithological Society, and numerous nest boxes are to be seen. Please don't leave the path and disturb the inhabitants! At the end of the path another gate leads you bacxk into Park-y-brain lane which will return you to the car park.

The Holy Well in a wooded cwm above Mamhilad

WALK FIVE
To the site of Capel Newydd

Over the ridge above the Goose and Cuckoo Inn to visit the site of a simple chapel once attached to Llanover and the first place of worship used by the people of Blaenavon.

3½ miles 5.6 kilometres

START: From the Goose and Cuckoo Inn (G.R. 290078)

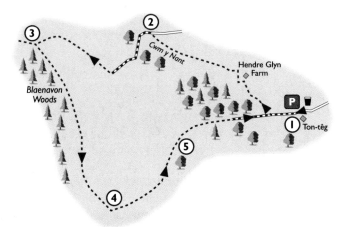

1. Walk up the road for a few hundred yards and take the farm drive on the right, leading to Hendre Glyn Farm, which nestles in the valley below. Just after crossing the chattering brook, go over a stile on the left and ascend the sloping field to reach a diagonal track directly above and turn left. Pass through a gate and observe the interesting conglomerate rocks scattered about the field. When the track flattens out, look to the right to see, near a farmhouse, a conical shaped construction. This is a beehive pigsty, once quite common in Wales.

2. Go through a gate and turn left along the road, which is followed over the ridge and cross a cattle grid. Ahead now, if visibility is good, will be seen the distinctive table-like summits of the Brecon Beacons. Follow the road towards Blaenavon to reach the site of Capel Newydd, just below a bend in the road.

The site of this ancient chapel is marked by an iron cross on a concrete plinth. It was Blaenavon's first church and is shown on a map published in 1600. At one time there was a stone in the graveyard bearing the date 1577, so the chapel was in existence for over three hundred years at the very least. The last sermon was preached here one Sunday in 1861. It was in Welsh, for no other language was used for services at Capel Newydd. In 1893 the abandoned building was demolished and the stone taken away for building St Paul's Church in Blaenavon.

A reconstruction of Capel Newydd by Michael Blackmore. This was Blaenavon's first Christian Church but was abandoned in 1861. The site is now marked by a simple iron cross.

3. Return up the road a short way and then turn right along a bridle path, just above a forestry plantation. The rutted track leads along a heather clad hillside to pass under some electricity wires. In the early years of the nineteenth century, this track was used by packhorses carrying iron ore to the Hanbury furnaces at Pontypool. These beasts of burden were operated in teams of twelve and each animal carried about three hundredweight.

To the right can be seen Mynydd Farteg Fawr and the community of Varteg. In the distance is Abersychan and the Bristol Channel may be seen far ahead, gleaming in the sunlight.

4. Turn left at a crossing of tracks (about 100 metres before a radio mast) and head up to a shallow col on the ridge, following a well trodden path which was once used by folk crossing the ridge bewteen Cwmavon and Llanover. On reaching the crest of the ridge, you may see ahead, the distinctive profile of Ysgyryd Fawr, the rounded hump of Graig Syffyrdin and the summit of Blorenge on the left.

5. Keep straight on and descend between stone walls, obviously built by skilled craftsmen. Go through a gate and continue beside a wall; then go down a stoney path to reach a gate. Keep straight on at the next junction of tracks and descend a tree-lined sunken lane to reach a gate. Then follow a cart track down to a tarmac road which leads back to the Goose and Cuckoo Inn.

WALK SIX
From the Goose and Cuckoo Inn

"Our list of Monmouthshire Taverns includes the 'Goose and Cuckoo', the 'Drum and Monkey', the 'Tippling Philosopher' and the 'Ramping Cat'.

Fred J. Hando

3½ miles 5.6 kilometres

START: From the Goose and Cuckoo Inn (G.R. 290073)

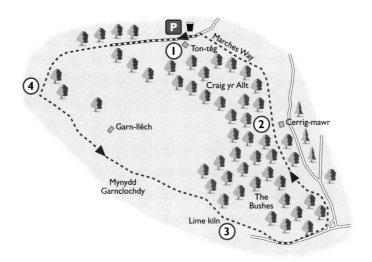

98

1. Walk down the road a short way to reach a gravel clearing on the right and follow the path through a conifer plantation to pass old beech trees with perhaps the occasional squirrel scuttling along branches. Keep straight on ignoring tracks on the right. There are good views over eastern Gwent through occasional gaps in the trees.

2. On reaching a crossroads just above a large house keep straight on up a stoney track to reach a gate. Now go immediately right to ascend a sunken lane (follow the right branch). This is a good example of some of the ancient routes to be found on this hillside. At the next junction follow the left hand branch of the track to reach a gate in a wall. On the other side follow a path up to the ridge directly above.

3. Follow a track along the north eastern side of the ridge with a stone wall on your right and passing old limestone quarries and the remains of a lime kiln. The track crosses a section of moorland which can be boggy in places, particularly after heavy rain. Keep just above the stone wall. An old Welsh longhouse will be seen perched on the hillside below. About ¼ mile beyond this building the wall bends sharply to the right.

4. Follow a track down between the stone walls, through a gate, across a track and down beside a stone wall to another gate. Keep straight on at the junction of tracks and down a sunken lane to reach another gate. Follow the tarmac road back to the Goose and Cuckoo Inn.

WALK SEVEN
Looking at Llanarth

A short circular walk providing good views of Llanarth Court, the ancestral home of the Herbert family.

2½ miles 4 kilometres

Start: Small layby near the entrance to Llanarth Churchyard (G.R. 375109)

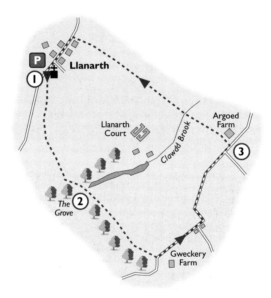

1. Just below the layby go over a stile by a fingerpost and turn right beside a hedge. Across to the left can be seen Llanarth Court. Head for a gateway in the bottom right corner of the field. Continue through the next field with a stream on the right of the path. Just to the right of a long rustic shed go over a stile to pass through woodland. On reaching the driveway to Llanarth Court, turn left and go over a little bridge. After about 50 yards turn right to follow a broad track leading through the trees to reach an impressive stone bridge spanning a linear ornamental lake. Pause on the centre of the bridge to enjoy a fine view of Llanarth Court, which is now a hospital.

2. Continue to reach a gate and keep straight on through the next field enjoying an even better view of Llanarth Court. This track takes you through very pleasant parkland with grazing animals and fine trees dotted around. A very gentle ascent leads up to a tall wooden gate set between stone pillars. Go through the gate and turn left along a tarmac road. On reaching 'Great Oak', keep straight on at a bend, leaving the road that you have been following.

3. Just before the red roofed Argoed Farm look out for a fingerpost on the left. Go through a gate and follow a fence down to another gate. Keep straight on through the field to cross a stone bridge over a brook and then bear slightly right to go through the next field, keeping a fence on your left. At the end of the fence go through a small gate and cross a bridge to immediately go through another gate. Keep straight on following the left hand side of the next field. In due course the path becomes a cart track. At the end of the field the track bends around to the right and then turns left to continue past agricultural buildings. On reaching a tarmac road turn left and walk through Llanarth village to reach your starting point near the church.

Llanarth Court, the ancient home of the Herbert family is now a hospital

CHRONOLOGY

1790   Harriet Waddington was born and died in the same year

1791   Francis Waddington was born

1793   Mary Ann Waddington was born, but died in infancy

1794   Emilia Waddington was born

1797   Benjamin Waddington purchased Ty Uchaf

1797   Matilda Waddington wasa born but died soon afterwards

1802   Augusta Waddington was born

1802   Benjamin Hall III was born

1819   Emelia Waddington died

1820   Benjamin Hall III matriculated at Christchurch, Oxford, but left without taking any degrees

1823   Augusta Waddington married Benjamin Hall III on December 4th

1831   Benjamin Hall becomes MP for the Monmouth boroughs

1833   The Cymdeithas Cymreigyddion y Fenni was founded

1834   Augusta Hall adopted the pseudonym Gwenynen Gwent (Bee of Gwent) and won a prize at the Cardiff Eisteddfod for an essay on the Welsh language

1837   Benjamin Hall becomes MP for Marylebone

1838   Benjamin Hall becomes a Baronet

1839   Hanover Chapel built

1846   Augusta, only surviving child of Augusta and Benjamin Hall, married Arthur Jones of Llanarth who later assumed the name of Herbert

1848   Benjamin Hall lost an eye in a shooting accident

1848   Death of Rev Thomas Price (Carnhuanawc)

1851   Ivor Caradoc Herbert was born

1854   Benjamin Hall is sworn in as a Member of the Privy Council

1855   Sir Benjamin Hall became Commissioner of Works (without a seat in the cabinet)

1859   Sir Benjamin Hall becomes Baron Llanover of Llanover and Abercarn

1861   Lord Llanover was sworn in as Lord-Lieutenant of Monmouthshire

1861   A portrait of Lady Llanover is presented by her husband to Llandovery College

1861   Lady Llanover edited the 'Autobiography and Correspondence of Mary Granville, Mrs Delaney'

1863   In July, Lord Llanover spoke in the upper house for the last time

1866   Death of Robert Jermain Thomas, a brave missionary from Llanover

1867   Lady Llanover edited a book containing illustrations by herself depicting Welsh female clothing

1867   Death of Lord Llanover at Great Stanhope Street, Mayfair at the age of 65

1876   Death of Francis Waddington

1888   Lady Llanover purchased the Coldbrook Estate

1896   Death of Lady Llanover aged 94

1917   Major General Sir Ivor Caradoc Herbert became Lord Treowen

1933   Death of Lord Treowen, grandson of Lady Llanover

1936   Demolition of Llanover Court

2003   The Lady Llanover Society was formed

THE LADY LLANOVER SOCIETY

This Society, officially launched on October 12th 2003 at Ty Uchaf aims to preserve the memory of Lady Llanover and her achievements. Details of the Society are available on-line at www.gwenynengwent.org.uk and www.lady llannover.org.uk

Over 600 people attended the launch of the Lady Llanover Society on 12th October 2003. Traditional dancing was performed by over 40 members of Cwmni Dawns Werin Caerdydd to the music of the Triple Harp Ensemble, y Rhes Ganol.

ACKNOWLEDGEMENTS

I am grateful to the following who have assisted me in the compiling of this book:-

Elizabeth Murray for reading the draft manuscript
and writing the Foreword

Ann Griffths and Marilyn Barrack for their comments on the draft
manuscript and suggestions for improvements

Richard Dowle for supplying two of the walk routes
and proof reading the descriptions of all the walks

David Perrott for drawing the route maps

Michael and Carol Langley of the Goose & Cuckoo Inn
for their hospitality and enthusiasm for the project

The numerous people that I encountered on my wanderings
in *Llanover Country* who helped me where possible
and expressed their interest in such a book being published.

BIBLIOGRAPHY

Bradney, J. A., *History of Monmouthshire*, Volume III, 1923

Coxe, William, *An Historical Tour in Monmouthshire*, Volume II, 1801

Evans, C.J.O., *Monmouthshire*, 1953

Hando, Fred, *Journeys in Gwent*,1951
    Out and About in Monmouthshire, 1958
    Here and There in Monmouthshire, 1964

Llanover, Lady, *The first Principles of Good Cookery and Recipes communicated by the Hermit of the Cell of St Gover*, 1867

Fraser, Maxwell, *West of Offa's Dyke*, 1958
    Numerous articles by Maxwell Fraser on the story of Lord and Lady Llanover (Newport Reference Library)

Newman John, *The Buildings of Wales – Gwent/Monmouthshire*, 2000

Phillips, Olive, *Monmouthshire*, 1951

Newspapers consulted: Abergavenny Chronicle, Pontypool Free Press and Monmouthshire Merlin